FLYING
BY THE SEAT OF YOUR PANTS

Mary Helen
Spread your wings!
Chis Waugh

"Learning the secret of flight from a bird was a good deal like learning the secret of magic from a magician. After you know what to look for you see things that you did not notice when you did not know exactly what to look for."

– Orville Wright

Flying

BY THE SEAT OF YOUR PANTS

A Hang Glider Pilot's View of Life

by Chris Waugh

Alberteen Press
Otter Rock, Oregon

First printing 2005.
ISBN 0-9763358-3-2
LCCN 2004116478

ATTENTION CORPORATIONS, UNIVERSITIES, COLLEGES, AND PROFESSIONAL ORGANIZATIONS: Quantity discounts are available on bulk purchases of this book for educational, gift purposes, or as premiums for increasing magazine subscriptions or renewals. Special books or book excerpts can also be created to fit special needs.

© 2005 Chris Waugh. Printed and bound in the United States of America. All rights reserved. No part of this book may be reproduced or transmitted in any form or by any means, electronic or mechanical, including photocopying, recording, or by an information storage and retrieval system — except by a reviewer who may quote brief passages in a review to be printed in a magazine, newspaper, or on the Web — without permission in writing from the publisher. For information, please contact:

Alberteen Press
165 3rd Street
Otter Rock, OR 97365

Illustrated by Harry Martin http://www.vcnet.com/~harry

Acknowledgments

Nothing happens in a vacuum. I want to thank the family, friends and colleagues who encouraged me, and held me accountable for completing this project. Scores of people helped in small ways. Others stand out in my mind, and I want to thank them individually:

To my husband, Bruce, whom I met hang gliding. For thirty years, he has been there to bounce ideas around with me, lending his detailed sense of reality to my creative imagination. Thanks for all the help and support while I was giving birth to this writing effort.

To my first draft editors, Alline McAlister, Dan & Jean Moore, Ruth Waugh, Joann DeMott and Janet Diaz — thanks for patiently plowing through my roughest initial efforts and relaying your perceptions back to me.

To Harry Martin, who created custom illustrations of the sport of hang gliding. Harry's work is great — check it out at http://www.vcnet.com/~harry.

To the professionals who put forth time and energy into the realization of my dream. Thanks to Rose Reed and Howard Shippey of Newport Lazerquick, and Carol Kersley. Your insights were invaluable.

And, of course, to my clients, readers and audiences, without whom my words would just blow away.

Table of Contents

FOREWORD
Dreams of Flight 1

INTRODUCTION
The Value of Winging It 5
Take the Pilot's Seat 11
Learn to Soar: Be Aware, Prepare & Dare 15

CHAPTER 1 – Be Aware of Yourself
Paying Attention 17
You – Think like a Pilot 20
Where You Are Heading 22
Your Focus & Perspective 24
Understand Your Limitations 26
Your Risk Tolerance 29
Pilot Responsibility 31

CHAPTER 2 – Be Aware of Others
Air Traffic – You're Not Alone Up There 35
Propel Yourself with Good Flight Instructors 37
What You Can Learn from Other Pilots 38
Keep Your Drivers Happy 43
About Spectators & "Wuffos" 44

CHAPTER 3 – Be Aware of Your Environment
Weather – the Changing Conditions 47
Meteorology vs. Micro-Meteorology 49
Turbulence, Instability & Opportunity 51
Forecasting the Future 54

CHAPTER 4 – Be Aware of the Dynamics
The Forces of Flight 57
The Attitude / Performance Connection 59

    Flight Speed & Momentum............................ 60
    Turning – You Have to Be Nimble 63

CHAPTER 5 – Prepare to Learn
    Contingency Factors................................. 67
    Take Flying Lessons 71
    Stretch Out of Your Comfort Zone 73
    Stay Current on the Basics 74

CHAPTER 6 – Prepare to Choose
    Uplifting Selections 77
    Trade-Offs in Hang Gliders 78
    Safety & Instruments 81
    Care in Handling & Maintenance..................... 84

CHAPTER 7 – Prepare to Practice
    Ground School..................................... 87
    Pre-Flight Procedures.............................. 88
    Flight Planning 92
    Logging Airtime 93

CHAPTER 8 – Dare to Fly
    Face the Future 95
    Commit to the Launch 97
    Perspectives in Flight 101
    The Landing Zone 107

FLYING HIGH
    Soar to New Heights 115
    Lending Wings to Others 117

    About The Author 120

FOREWORD

"Travelers are always discoverers, especially those who travel by air. There are no signposts in the sky to show that a man has passed that way before."

— Ann Morrow Lindberg

Dreams of Flight

In my earliest dreams, I twirled around until my full skirt somehow generated lift and I floated slowly upward. (Things like that make sense in dreams.) I would hover thirty or forty feet off the ground. Looking down on my neighborhood, I could see the little aluminum trailers with white picket fences around each one. I could see fathers working on their cars, mothers weeding their flowerbeds, and my friends playing in their yards.

They were confined to the ground.

And they all saw me floating up there. They looked up at me with their mouths agape. Of course, they were amazed.

I could fly!

But it was just a vivid dream.

I think I inherited the flying bug from my Grandpa

Flanigan. Since I can remember, he was a pilot and always had an airplane. One was a Luscome 8A. I remember how he had to "hand prop" it to start the engine. Grabbing the prop, he wound his body up like a baseball pitcher, lifting a leg to help with the momentum as he unwound and flung the prop hard enough to start it turning. Sometimes it took him two or three tries to get it to spin on its own, and start the motor. Finally, when it did, he'd duck around the prop, hop up into the cockpit, roar down the dirt airstrip, gaining speed, take off and fly!

Grandpa Flanigan and his Luscome 8A

I was awestruck. I was with him, but only in spirit.

My mother would never let me go for a ride with him, although I would plead with her. When I was a teenager I was finally deemed old enough and I got to go up in the air with him.

The day he took me for a flight in his PT-2 Trainer was the day I got a new perspective on life. First, I noticed the change in dimension. Everything was so small — miniature, really. The houses, the cars, and the people — they all looked like little toys. I remember seeing a vehicle and thinking that the person driving it probably thought he had some big problem. But from my new vantage point, I knew differently. His problem was teensy, just like he was. It was just a matter of perspective.

That meant my problems were just as small, if seen from a different perspective. It was just a short flight, but my vantage point changed forever.

Grandpa crashed that plane in 1970. He and his passenger both survived. I remember he was hospitalized with multiple broken bones in his head. The doctors put him back together, and his jaw was wired shut. Two days later, he was home. I remember he was mad because all he could eat was baby food. That episode kept the risk of flying in the front of my mind.

Yet I still dreamed about it.

When I was in college, my boyfriend took parachuting lessons. I thought he was so lucky. He got to go on a plane ride and jump out! I wanted to take lessons, too. However, because I was only nineteen, I needed "parental consent." I was thwarted. My mother refused because she was worried that I could get hurt. My father refused because he thought I was nuts.

The dreams continued.

Years later I was a bank teller. My meager salary, however, barely paid the bills. I thought that any flying I would be doing was going to have to stay confined to my dreams.

Then I heard about a new sport called hang gliding. Before I even knew what it was, I knew that I would love it.

For one thing, I could afford it. The manager of the bank where I worked loaned me eighty percent of the $630 purchase price for my hang glider. I remember he also made me buy credit life insurance for the loan. He said he wanted that loan paid off if I killed myself in my new contraption.

Plus, I was old enough that I didn't need consent from my parents. I could hang glide if I wanted to.

I would have my own kite, only mine would be without a string constantly holding me to the ground.

Since that time, my early dreams have been a reality. I can fly by the seat of my pants. And from that experience, I have seen bigger parallels that lead to the philosophies in this book.

My first flying lessons were in a hang glider. But I learned I could stretch different wings. I launched several businesses, and flew them successfully. I lifted my voice and learned to sing in harmony.

I even challenged my self-imposed limitation and fear of writing by deciding to write about this new perspective.

After the many small steps and setbacks that it takes to undertake any adventure, this book is complete.

Sure, there was turbulence on the way, but the journey has been great. I've experienced things I never thought possible. You can too.

This book is your pilot's manual.

INTRODUCTION

"It is not the strongest of the species that survive, nor the most intelligent, but the one most responsive to change."

— Charles Darwin

The Value of Winging It

The idea of flying by the seat of your pants didn't always have a bad rap. The term originated in the early days of human flight. Pilots felt their aircraft move in response to their action at the controls and the wind conditions. These feelings literally came through the seat of their pants. They maneuvered nimbly "on the fly" according to how they interpreted those changing sensations.

They were venturing into the unknown — so, that's how they had to do it.

These days, navigating on the fly is often impractical and avoided. Aviation has technology. Most aircraft have engines for power, sophisticated instruments and strict flight regulations. Pilots document very specific flight plans. Half of the airplanes even have an autopilot! They know exactly where they are going.

Today, people associate winging it with a haphazard approach to life. It seems flippant, or disrespectful, to make it up as you go along — not to have a plan and strategies. It feels unorganized. How can you possibly succeed that way?

After all, we were taught much differently. "Plan your work, and work your plan." "Your goals should be precise, measurable, written, and dated." "Know your destination and then map out your journey to get there." And, "Always keep your eyes on the goal."

Those maxims sound too much like a stereotypical goal-setting-for-success seminar. We are told that our plans and maps will give us control over our journey. But do they? Do these old maxims lead to success?

When we're making life choices, or long-range business decisions, those old tactics are only moderately successful. This is why:

- *Our world is space, time and energy.*
- *We don't always have a specific goal.*
- *We are time-pressed and stressed.*
- *We are overlooking opportunities.*
- *Plans don't always work!*

Let's examine each of these realities more closely:

Our world is space, time and energy.

A concrete world is easy to envision and seems logical and secure. It is flat. It is two-dimensional. We can map it. We can plan how to go from Point A to Point B. Everything is fixed, stable. It's reassuring.

But that's only one snapshot of reality. And it's like trying to find the end of the rainbow — there is no there.

The real world is much different. Our environment is space and energy. It is three-dimensional. It is full of invisible currents and turbulence, like the wind. And, like the wind, it is also full of opportunities. It's moving. It's always changing. It's scary.

The business world is more than two-dimensional, too. You cannot confine all of the variables of an organization with structure, although many people try. A business is fluid, always in motion. And, like any relationship, business is full of emotion. Both are comprised of humans, doing the best they can. They're all flying by the seat of their pants.

The future is uncertain; you can't see it. You can't map it, or specify a Point B. If you try to specify it, it may be gone by the time you reach it. In reality, though, even our goals are moving targets. By the time we reach them, their impact may be gone. We might find that we didn't want them after all, or maybe times have changed, or the goals themselves have changed. On the other hand, maybe we have changed.

Planning rarely allows for the fluidity of the future.

We don't always have a specific goal.

We've been taught to plan our work and work our plan. We're supposed to map out our journey. How can we get there without knowing where we're going, right?

Well, maps are useful if we are going to a specific place, like Paris to find love. Or Nashville to be a country star. Or the Oregon coast to fly a kite.

Maps work in a two-dimensional world where our destination is fixed and known. But what if we're not exactly sure where we're going? What if we don't have a clear image of our destination? What if our goals are somewhat vague?

In major life decisions, this is true much of the time. All we can do is set off in a direction, hoping to clarify the goal as we approach it.

We are time-pressed and stressed.
We're moving at the speed of life. We're frequently too busy and bombarded to set goals and plans as we've learned. We don't always have the time for the process. And we stress out about that.

Meanwhile, challenges are continually blindsiding us from all directions.

When we try to analyze every incident and control our journey, life leaves us exhausted and frustrated.

We want stability. We yearn for the good old days. We want things to get back to normal (whatever that is, or was.) We're swept up in the motion. Instead of winging it effectively, we thrash against the current or drift with it aimlessly. Either way, it's not effective.

We are suspicious of the invisible environment we journey through and apprehensive of the future.

We are overlooking opportunities.
Since we're encouraged to set goals, sometimes we set a specific target too soon. By focusing solely on the goal, we are filtering out other, perhaps better, options. Instead of identifying opportunities as we fly through life, we become blind to them.

To make matters worse, we tend to prepare for our goals, but not the other possibilities that we will encounter. If we identify an opportunity, but are not prepared for it, it doesn't wait for us. It's gone.

So we have to be aware of an opportunity, be prepared to take advantage of it, and dare to be nimble. Plus, we have to do it all on the fly.

Plans don't always work.

Remember when you were young, trying to decide on a life or career path? (Some of us still haven't decided.) What were you going to be?

Well, were you right? Did you see yourself exactly where you are now? Did you envision your current position?

Probably not.

How did you successfully arrive without knowing where you were going? You took advantage of opportunities as you became aware of them, and avoided perceived threats. You made the best of the conditions you encountered along the journey. You flew by the seat of your pants.

Think of the ability to wing it as an acquired skill. That's how I like to think of it — like when I fly my hang glider.

Let me take you on a flight:

I pick up my hang glider. It weighs sixty pounds and the wingspan is over thirty feet. I keep the nose pointed directly into the wind, and always hold the wings level. I carry it over to the two thousand foot high launch, and set the glider down with its nose just over the edge. I hook myself into the wing and double check everything.

I can't "see" the wind — the environment through which I will be flying. But, I can feel the effect of it. It's coming right up the launch and it brushes against my face. I turn my head from side to side until my nose points directly into the oncoming wind. The wing is heavy and cumbersome, and the wind tugs on the glider. I have to work to keep it level as I stand there holding it. As I gaze over the edge, I am aware of the wind indicators — the flags, trees, birds and airborne gliders.

I wait for smooth, straight, uphill wind flow.

Finally, everything feels right and it's time to launch. I run! I keep a level glider attitude while I build the momentum to flight speed within a few short steps. Suddenly, I am creating lift and my glider starts to fly. It plucks my running feet right off the ground!

In the air, I adjust myself comfortably in my cocoon-like harness. My plan today is to fly around and land in Farmer Fred's Field, which is the normal landing area. My driver will meet me there with my vehicle.

The air seems smooth at first, but soon I notice that pockets of turbulence are everywhere. Some are small and others bigger. There are gusts, updrafts, downdrafts, rotors, and, in today's case, thermals rising. I recognize the feeling of those hot air bubbles, and I notice cumulus clouds forming high above me. Even though it's a struggle to maneuver, I shift my weight to fly the glider directly into a big and turbulent thermal. I turn tight circles in it, staying within that bubble and I start to rise with it.

Within a few minutes, I climb almost two thousand feet in altitude. That was a good thermal!

I look around. My horizons have expanded. The world is spread out below me.

The clouds above me indicate that there are more thermals forming today — more potential for lift. More opportunities.

I decide to change my flight plan and wave goodbye to Farmer Fred's Field. I decide to fly cross country, and a couple hours and many thermals later, I've logged thirty miles. Thanks to cellular technology, I speed dial my driver with my new destination. My retrieval vehicle is waiting with cold refreshments on the tailgate when I land.

Now *that* is flying by the seat of your pants.

A hang glider has no cockpit, no dash board or high-tech flight controls. There is no power other than your own brains and energy. It is a pure form of aviation, and winging it is still the only way to do it. You keep your senses and your options open. Search for lift and take advantage of the opportunities you find.

Note that the opportunity to soar higher is in the flight, not the landing. The possibilities come from the journey, not the destination. The potential is in the air, not on the ground.

Don't be afraid to fly in the face of conventional wisdom. Learn how to fly by the seat of your pants, to wing it, to succeed on the fly. This is a skill you'll need in the real world, and this book can help you get it.

These replacement adages are quite different from the established ones: Be aware and prepared, and make a general flight plan. Your goals don't have to be specific. Your destination matters less than the quality of the flight. Keep your eyes open for opportunities.

You can learn to adapt and maneuver in change and uncertainty. Better yet — you can learn to take advantage of it.

Take the Pilot's Seat

You've been there all along.

Nobody was given an owner's manual at birth. You didn't take lessons to participate in the sport of life. You simply ventured out, and tackled the problems that blew your way. You made it all up as you went along. You did the best you could, or anyway, you thought so.

That's called flying by the seat of your pants, and you do it all the time. We all do.

What if you knew how to do it better? What if you could take off and wing it effectively? What if you could identify more opportunities on the way? And, what if you were better prepared to take advantage of them?

Learning to fly hang gliders, and then flying them for decades, has been an education for me. The obvious lessons involve the details of flying hang gliders. But, the larger life lessons have been even more valuable.

Flying gave me the discipline and techniques that expanded my horizons. Those skills transferred to many other things I tried.

I mentioned that I was a bank teller when I first learned to fly. My career was on autopilot. I had no long-range plan. I didn't have or take the time for thinking and preparation much past my next paycheck. Like many of my friends, I was running just to keep up with yesterday. And, I wasn't getting anywhere.

Then I decided to apply some hang gliding concepts to my career.

I looked for opportunities in the bank, and started to prepare myself for a move up the ladder. I made lateral changes, and then enrolled in the management training program. I was eventually making business loans. From my banking background, I became aware of my love for businesses. I understood what made them financially tick, but I wanted to get more into the leadership of the organization.

I spent the next sixteen years managing businesses, and increased my experience and knowledge working through other people. I developed philosophies about motivation that contributed to the success of those organizations. With that base, I became aware of my entrepreneurial spirit. So, I launched my own company, reNvision, which specializes in delivering new perspectives. Now, I lend wings to people's success through keynote speeches, training workshops, writing and consulting.

Maybe I would have grown the same way without learning to fly. But, I don't think so.

I think you can learn a lot about life from hang gliding.

When I told people that I was going to buy a hang glider, they looked at me like when I told them I was going to start my new business. I know those looks — they are quite similar. At first, their look was amused. They were entertained by the idea.

"Self-confidence is the result of a successfully survived risk."

– Jack Gibb

After they realized that I was serious, their look became more ominous. They told me that they knew someone who broke an arm (or died) hang gliding. They knew of businesses that had failed. They were fearful of the risk I was assuming.

"What if you can't hold on to the hang glider?"

"What if you hit a down draft or bad air?" "What if the glider falls apart, and you can't get away from your glider to throw your parachute?" "Do you have a death wish?"

"What if your new business doesn't take off?" "Remember, eighty percent of businesses fail during their

Flying by the Seat of Your Pants

first year or two." "What if you have a marketing problem, or inadequate cash flow?" "Your business failure can take you right down the drain with it."

"You'll have to carry that failure around with you like a scar from a compound fracture."

Yet secretly, I think my friends were thrilled at the thought of actually taking flight, or launching a business.

Learning to fly can be a great confidence builder. One old boss I had used his tirades to intimidate people and make his point. He went through managers like toothpicks. I stood up to him, though, so I usually got more than my share of his venting. One time he asked me, "Why aren't you afraid of me?" I laughed and reminded him that I had successfully run off a cliff and completed a cross-country flight in my hang glider on the past weekend. After that adventure, what was his yelling going to do to me?

When you learn to fly on your own, you become more confident, decisive, focused, fit and free. Luckily, you can learn basic flying concepts without ever touching a hang glider, much less approaching a cliff with it strapped to your back. There are parallels between flying lessons and issues you face in your life and work every day.

As a pilot, you'll have a reputation of calm control under pressure. You'll take command of your flight and the environment, and calculate the risks involved. Then you'll decide where to go and when to launch. You'll be decisive. You'll take responsibility for your actions. You'll be nimble — sometimes in a split second, you'll change directions. You'll respond to new opportunities.

As boundaries disappear and horizons broaden, your world will become a little smaller. Your vantage point will change. No longer too close to the forest to see the trees, you will see both the forest and the trees. As a hang glider pilot, you are free to go in the direction you want. You'll soar with hawks, falcons, seagulls and eagles, and you'll routinely view nature at her most spectacular.

Maybe you don't want to learn to fly, but you are doing it anyway. You are already winging it. If you want control over your flight, start your flying lessons.

You are in the pilot seat. You can't step out of it, because you are doing the flying! You are the one living your life. But until you think of it as flying, you never learn to fly.

Now it's time.

Learn to Soar:
Be Aware, Prepare & Dare

There are three overlapping components to flying by the seat of your pants. Be aware, prepare and dare. That's all there is to it. The rest of this book covers them.

First, you have to be aware. This step requires a keen insight and level of understanding. Most people don't have their awareness refined to a high enough level. You will learn to use your brain better. This is where you will start, and spend a great deal of time. In fact, this is where you'll spend most of the time — being aware.

The next step is to prepare. You will be navigating through an unfamiliar medium — the future. It is turbulent with threats and opportunities. You will prepare physically and mentally for the voyage, and understand the dynamics and the variables. It involves learning and stretching.

Many would-be pilots stop there.

Take the third step — dare. It's the hardest part. But, the dare is where the growth happens. The dare is the launch on the journey.

Learning to wing it is not a linear process. It's not like a race with a start and a finish. You don't go through these three steps once and have it completed. Learning is not a simple cycle, either. If it were, you'd be retracing the same steps repeatedly. Learning is more like an upward spiral. You are working your way up — as I do when I'm turning in the core of a rising thermal. And just like that thermal, there are bumps and dips as you rise. Learning is turbulent. Sometimes you have setbacks, and sometimes you gain more than you thought was possible.

Sometimes you can't even tell if you're making any progress at all. But if you stand back, you'll see that overall, you are.

Be aware, prepare and dare. These are the three steps for flying by the seat of your pants. It's the way to soar a hang glider, and its how you succeed in the real world.

"Flexible is much too rigid;
in aviation you have to be fluid."

– Verne Jobst

CHAPTER 1 – BE AWARE OF YOURSELF

> *"The first step toward change is awareness.*
> *The second step is acceptance."*
>
> – Nathaniel Branden

Paying Attention

Understanding the world takes constant observation. Look at yourself, your comrades, and your environment with an effort to see objectively. The more you observe, the more you see. The more you see, the more you understand. The more you understand, the better you can maneuver on the fly.

When I managed an aquarium, I remember being informed that two of our guests had been hitch hiking across the United States. This happy couple, however, was blind! My first reaction was that all our marine exhibits were behind glass — how could they see them? I introduced myself and started talking about some of the species of sea life we had there. We had a "touch and feel" tank and I guided them to it. Meanwhile, they told me about their adventures crossing the country. They told me that as they entered a town, they could identify the different fast food joints — by smell! They could tell the difference between McDonald's, Burgerville, Arctic Circle and Burger King.

Then, my ignorance came rushing out ahead of my words. Wow! I exclaimed that since they were blind, their sense of smell must be really sharp.

No, they gently chided me. Everyone's sense of smell is the same. But not everyone is equally aware.

That was a good lesson.

Being aware is the most important part. It yields the best results for the smallest effort.

Being aware is also the hardest part. When I facilitate planning sessions for management teams or boards of directors, I notice how they tend to skip lightly over this part. They want to briefly review the mission statement and immediately begin to set their goals and develop plans and strategies. But if they don't understand their situation clearly, how can they set good goals? And if they don't set good goals, how do they prepare? How do they succeed?

Don't minimize this first step. In fact, I don't think it's possible to be too aware! Awareness has four aspects: yourself, others, and the laws of weather and flight.

First, know yourself. It can be most difficult, but you need to understand what makes you tick. Do this with a great deal of respect. Realize your motivations and utilize your strengths, and based on them, set a direction.

Next, recognize that other people are on different, but no less important, flight paths. Respect them, too. If you're working together in business or on a team, those flight paths need to be parallel. Everyone has to be aware of the group purpose. Every must be focused on the same heading and going in the same direction.

Third, pay attention to the climate around you — which way the wind blows, so to speak. Respect Mother Nature. You live and work in this environment. It's the future. You'll be looking for opportunities.

Finally, you'll want to understand the dynamics of flight, so you know how to take advantage of the potential you find. You'll need to be an expert at maneuvering.

When you fly, look around — up, down, above and below you. Anticipate; look for invisible signs of lift. Watch the birds — they are expert pilots. Somehow, they intuitively know where the best lift is. If their wings are stretched out and their feathers extended, they are in light lift. They are milking every bit of opportunity that they experience. Or if their wings are tucked in at the shoulders, they are in strong wind. Penetration is difficult, and they reduce the surface of their wing lest the wind blows them out of control.

Thermal lift is illusive, just like the future. So use all your senses. There are physical tugs on your wing. The breeze blows over your skin. Watch for clues. Smell them. Survey the trees. Look at flags or smoke. Watch other hang gliders. Even though the wind isn't visible, there are always many indicators.

Opportunities in life and work are like that. They, too, are invisible, but they usually have signs. Watch other people, other teams or other businesses. See what is working and what isn't. You'll get an inkling. Use your intuition. Develop the foresight to see opportunities, or you'll be seeing them in hindsight. And if that happens, learn from your hindsight!

Let's explore in greater detail each of the elements of being aware.

You – Think Like A Pilot

If you are like the rest of us, you probably have too close of a view of yourself. That is why your life seems larger than life. Your problems are bigger. Your failures are bigger. Your needs are more urgent. Your fears are worse. As humans, we can be so dramatic!

On the other hand, maybe you are the opposite. Maybe, you know everyone else better than you know yourself. You haven't taken the time to know yourself as a person. What interests you? What motivates you? What do you avoid at all costs? Why do you react to certain situations the way you do?

You have an autopilot function, just like many airplanes. On one hand, it's a wonderful convenience. It allows you to do repetitive tasks without conscious thought. What would you do if you had to concentrate and focus on driving to work, opening a desk drawer, picking up a fork or tying your shoes? Your autopilot saves you time and energy. Your mind wants to help, and your autopilot kicks in as soon as possible.

"There are three things extremely hard: steel, a diamond, and to know one's self."

– Benjamin Franklin

Sometimes it's so automatic that you don't think about whether or not you should be using it. Unfortunately, many people fly through their whole lives on autopilot. Be careful of this tendency. Use your mind on purpose. Decide when to let the autopilot take control, and when you should be in charge.

Figure out what's important — what matters? What do you like to do? What are you good at? Be aware of where you are and where you want to go.

Reconsider your self image. Is it respectful? Is it rational, or judgmental and full of criticism? Do you feel you have to be perfect to create a healthy image of yourself?

As a pilot, you have many key areas to be aware of yourself. What excites you? Where do you want to go? How do you see your world? What limitations do you have, and what self-imposed limitations do you subscribe to? How is your tolerance of risk? Do you take full responsibility for your results?

The point here is not to judge yourself as much as it is to inventory yourself, and really understand yourself. If you know your own values, strengths, weaknesses, delights and fears, you can accommodate and utilize them more effectively.

Emphasize your strengths and delights. Some people spend too much time trying to improve their weaknesses and manage their fears. This is a human tendency but a waste of time. Focus on the positive. You get more for your energy that way, and you'll have more fun doing it.

You are rare and individual. You are special. You are evolving. Be kind and objective, and understand yourself. Let's explore some different aspects of this self-awareness.

Where You Are Heading

Your heading is the "why" of what you do. It takes a lot of introspection. It takes ongoing study of your own personality and motivations. It isn't easy, but it is extremely important.

Maybe you just want to be the best parent you can be, or the best kid. You could want to be a great corporate spouse. Or, boss. Of course, you have to determine what the best means to you. You might want to balance other aspects of your life, like improve your health. Or, develop your spiritual side. Or, awaken your artistic potential. Or, any combination of the above. Only you can decide what success means to you.

Why do you fly? Why do you live? Why do you work? What is your mission, passion or purpose? What gift do you have that you could share with the world? Maybe it's your creativity, or your ability to build, cook, lead or teach.

The stronger your awareness of the why, the more easily you can build momentum in that direction. Tentative people tend to drift. Aware people are more determined. If you are determined, you'll be focused.

Are you trying to prove something? If so, to whom? And for what reasons? Knowing the answers will affect the results of your flight, your work and your life.

We are all motivated by different factors. Some of us like quiet. Others get bored with quiet. Some of us like many people around us. Others get overwhelmed when there are too many people around us. There is no right or wrong answer. Don't judge yourself — just know yourself.

You can fool everyone else about your intentions, but you can't fool yourself. Your own intentions affect you most of all, even if they're subconscious. That's why they say you hurt yourself when you try to hurt other people. You also help yourself when you strive to help others. And being aware of your intentions will help you clarify your heading.

I remember a few hang glider pilots who flew for questionable reasons. Maybe they flew because their friends did. Maybe they felt they had to prove something. Maybe they had a death wish. I could always see it in their eyes when I helped them at launch. They were scared. They weren't happy. They weren't having fun. Why were they doing it? These people weren't successful pilots. Some of them didn't live long, either.

"If a man does not know what port he is steering for, no wind is favorable to him."

– Seneca

I also know people who pursued their occupations out of lust for power or money, instead of a genuine enjoyment of their work. Or people who drifted into the work they do, and feel they are trapped. But they aren't really aware of their true feelings. How can these people be successful, balanced or happy?

What gets you excited when you wake up in the morning? What do you like to do for the sheer joy of it?

On the other hand, what do you dread? What absolutely repels you?

Some of us are motivated by rewards and others are motivated by fears. Do you aim for the positive, or veer away from the negative? Both strategies work, and you have probably experienced both. But, you have a predominant style. Which is it?

Head for your passion, your inspiration. Give your gift. Once you have chosen a heading, your autopilot can be of service.

My business, reNvision, is about taking another look. I want you to reNvision yourself often. I have gradually discovered my own quirky life philosophies, and my passion for helping other people. My own evolution into my business has been a result of that awakening awareness.

"Vision is the art of seeing things invisible."

– Jonathan Swift

Your heading is less about goal setting than it is about understanding your values, your mission, and setting a direction in life. Be aware of what motivates you. Which heading will you take?

Your Focus & Perspective

Besides understanding your heading, how do you see your world? You have many choices of focus and perspective, and it is important that you choose them wisely.

By flying, I was allowed to separate myself from existence, as I knew it. I had no string holding my glider to the world. I was above it all. I could see the wholeness of life — how it all was connected. I had a brand new vantage point — a fresh perspective.

We learn to focus. Our perspective evolves from it. Consider babies; they can't focus at first. They stare — drooling mouths wide open — at everything, or maybe at nothing. There is an overwhelming amount of stimulus for them to process. They learn to filter their world. You would have probably gone crazy if you didn't learn to focus. By focusing on one thing, however, be aware that you are filtering out another.

Pay attention, because you pay for your attention. A friend with whom I took beginner hang gliding lessons only lasted about a year in the sport. One sunny day we were at the beach, practicing on the sand dune. She flew right into the only log on the beach. She landed sitting on the log, with her glider perched above her. When she didn't move, I hurried over to see what was wrong. She was wincing, and said that she thought she had broken her leg. As it turned out, she broke both of her legs, an ankle, and her back. Later, she told me that she had focused on that log, hoping to avoid it. Instead, she flew her glider straight into it, and it was her last flight. After she healed, she took up scuba diving.

The negatives and fears in life can demand your attention, but use caution. Maintain your control over your focus or else you'll fly right to where you do not want to be. It's like when you hit ice while driving, and you start to slide. They recommend that you focus and steer in the direction you want to go, not look to where you're sliding.

Be careful that your autopilot doesn't control your

focus and perspective. Vision is your dominating sense, so direct it properly. Focusing takes practice. There are many distractions out there. Be careful.

Keep changing your focus. Keep your perspective flexible. When you focus on one thing, you might miss something else that is important.

Finally, be careful of focusing excessively on the past or the future. Keep your mind in the present. It is the only thing that you can possibly control. Don't focus on a mistake you made a minute ago; otherwise, you will not be paying attention to where you are now, or what lies just ahead.

I learned that in singing. If I hit a wrong note, it was easy to reprimand myself for it. Meanwhile, the rest of the song was going on, but I wasn't focusing on singing it well. The results weren't melodious.

Finally, look at yourself from different vantage points. Be inside yourself looking out — that's easy. We all spend most of our lives there. Then try to be someone else looking at you. That gives you another view. Try being different people, friends and enemies as well. Imagine what you look like through their perspective. And, look at your situation from a distance, from a bird's eye view. You'll be more detached and impartial, and you'll understand the big picture.

You'll be more aware.

Understand Your Limitations

Can we really be anything we want? We are encouraged to think so. We'd love to believe it, but secretly we know: No.

I remember when I was about four, imagining what I'd be when I grew up. I told my mother I'd be a movie star, and later the President. She was always very encouraging, saying that if I worked very hard at it, I could be anything I wanted. Before long, I had a new idea. I told her that I was going to be an Indian princess. She sat me down and told me that I would never be able to be an Indian princess. I was not Indian, like the one in my coloring book, with long shiny black hair. I was not a princess, either.

That was an early lesson about limitations. People have them. Everyone has different ones. Our limitations are often barriers, but sometimes we can work around them.

However, we're not always willing to work hard enough to achieve a particular dream. That was the case for me in all those early career ideas. I guess I didn't want to be a movie star or the President badly enough to do what it would have taken to achieve that level.

"Too many people overvalue what they are not, and undervalue what they are."

– Malcom S. Forbes

There is a typical pilot: five feet ten inches tall and one hundred seventy pounds. Male. Fit. Macho. What if you don't fit the profile? Most people don't fit a typical profile of whatever they are trying to do, because a profile is just an average. You can still do it, though.

Flying by the Seat of Your Pants

You can still fly. I have seen paraplegics fly hang gliders (they get help launching.) I was a woman in man's sport. I found out that it is OK to be a girl! However, women approach flying quite differently.

For a man, the gear to body weight ratio is about one-half. For me it is more like two-thirds. In addition, a woman is not typically as strong in the upper body as a man. I had to learn to finesse the glider instead of using brute strength. I could not be as aggressive, or as macho.

Everybody looks the same when they land, too. They all have a harness and helmet covering most of them. When I'd remove my helmet, I sometimes felt like a poster child for a birth announcement. I'd hear the people say, "It's a girl!"

I was aware of my physical limitations. But, I had desire and I could see how my light weight and agility might compensate somewhat for my physical weakness. In that case, my desire was strong enough to overcome my limitations.

But, we also develop many self-imposed limitations over our lifetimes. Sometimes they are fostered in our childhood. Many times, we keep them with us forever. But, breaking through them is the key to progress. Learning to fly gave me confidence, and made me think I could do other things that I didn't think possible. I began to challenge my other boundaries.

A teacher told me in the fifth grade not to sing in the chorus — I was told just to stand still. I was told again in high school that my body and facial shape were too thin to be a singer. I bought into that concept for years. Most of the women singers that I could think of were rotund and I was skinny. At some point, finally, I questioned them. I joined a start-up chorus, figuring that they were desperate for members and I could start with them from scratch. I have enjoyed singing in harmony groups since that time.

As a business manager, I always hired someone to write for me — press releases, articles, and marketing material. I always thought that I could talk, but that I could not write. I told myself that, and I told everyone else. Now, I've decided to risk the consequences by doing it anyway — I've decided to reNvision myself as a writer.

Consider your limitations. Which ones are real? Which ones are self-imposed? Can you tell the difference?

You can box yourself in with self-imposed limitations. If you don't question their validity, you'll make them come true.

Your Risk Tolerance

We each have a different threshold for risk. Some people fear dentists, doctors, eating worms, seeing blood, or crowds. The list is different for each of us. We each assign an acceptable level of risk to the things we do.

As a fledgling hang glider pilot, I had an old framed sepia print that hung in my living room. It was a 1930s picture of an airplane, crashed thirty feet up in a lone oak tree. The pilots head was bent forward; it was unclear if he had survived the impact. The caption, attributed to British Captain A. G. Lamplugh, read, "Aviation in itself is not inherently dangerous. But to an even greater degree than the sea, it is terribly unforgiving of any carelessness, incapacity or neglect."

That phrase was, and still is, profound to me. You

"Good judgment comes from experience and experience comes from bad judgment."

— *Unknown*

can't see the air through which you fly. You can't see the future, either. You are flying by the seat of your pants, and there is no room for carelessness, incapacity or neglect.

Risk tolerance is not a constant factor; it evolves and changes as you do.

A woman who once worked with me was repulsed by anything gooey — like slime, drool or blood. A few years later, when she had two children, I asked her about her gooey tolerance. She laughed and admitted that she was immune to gooey stuff since she had children. She had gotten over it.

When teenagers first learn to drive, they have a low risk tolerance. Every other car, pedestrian, and stoplight causes excess concern. Soon, however, their tolerance swings to the other extreme. I used to jump my old Rambler American by driving it downhill fast over the peak of an intersection. It was my way of flying at the time! It was stupid now that I think of it, but it was fun then. I was in the immortal stage of life, and had a high risk tolerance for driving.

There is a fine line between success and failure. You'll make mistakes, and sometimes get away with it. If you have no negative repercussions, you might assume you'll always get away with it. You might relax your process. Then you make the same mistake again. The odds are that this will catch up with you. I was lucky — I stopped "flying" my Rambler before I killed myself or someone else!

Our risk tolerance affects the choices we make and those choices affect our results.

Pilot Responsibility

When hang gliding, you make a myriad of choices that affect your flight. You choose your fellow pilots. You choose your equipment. You choose your launch timing. You maintain your equipment, or you choose not to bother. You choose where to fly, and make all the minute corrections to get there. You decide how much risk is acceptable and act accordingly. You choose where you land, and how to set up your approach.

The myriad of choices you make in life affect its quality, too. You choose to focus on your education and which school to attend. You choose the classes to take and your major course of study. You choose your friends and lovers. You choose your work ethic. You choose how you spend your money. You choose your diet and your health regimen.

Self-responsibility is about accepting the choices that you make. You are not the victim of your circumstances, but the creator of them. Understanding that is empowering.

This concept is easy when you have a good flight, or if you are successful at anything. However, when things backfire, it's not so easy to admit your poor choices. That is how a victim mentality is born — blaming something outside of yourself when things go awry.

One winter day, a group of us gathered at a flying site to check out the potential. The wind was light, so most of us decided not to attempt a launch. Except one pilot, who decided he could clear the oak trees just off launch, even though the wind direction wasn't right. He said he had made it before. Well this time, he didn't clear the trees. He crashed high into an oak tree fifty feet off the ground. It took us most of the day to get him out of his predicament.

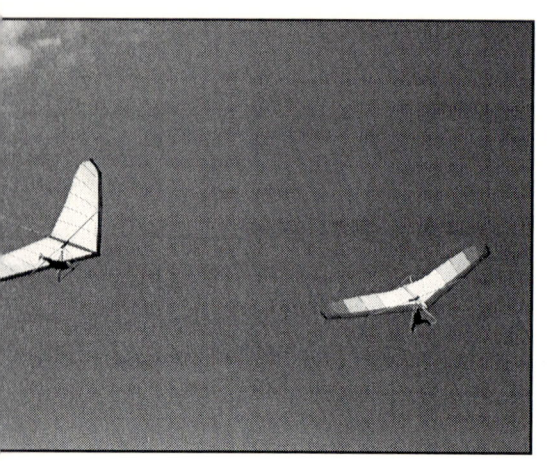

"Too many people are thinking of security instead of opportunity. They seem more afraid of life than death."

— James F. Byrnes

He blamed it on a downdraft. We knew better. Pilot error is always to blame. That's because the pilot judged the risk and decided to proceed.

I thought I was an expert investor in the 1990s. Didn't we all? The market was going crazy. My portfolio was yielding higher than average returns, and I thought I was a genius. Then, all too soon, when my high-tech portfolio took a dreaded turn for the worse, I blamed it on the market. Then I had to take responsibility. It wasn't the market's fault!

Thinking like a victim is easy to do. But, unfortunately, you don't learn anything that way. If you don't learn, you're apt to repeat.

Take responsibility for your choices, if you want to learn and succeed. Every choice you make affects you — even the choices that nobody notices. You choose your character, and your ethics. By doing so, you choose your fate. Our current situation is the sum total of all the choices we've made to date.

We are bombarded by choices. Choices make us think, unless we make them on autopilot. Choices made on autopilot can become unconscious bad habits.

Don't choose the comfortable rather than change. Don't choose to stay on the ground, rather than risk flight. However, it is choosing to launch that creates the possibility to soar.

All these aspects of being aware gives us insights into ourselves, and more control of our future.

CHAPTER 2 – BE AWARE OF OTHERS

> *"We should expect the best and the worst of mankind, as from the weather."*
>
> – Marquis De Vauvenargues

Air Traffic – You're Not Alone Up There

As a pilot, you're alone out there in your responsibility, but you're not flying alone. Your spatial environment surrounds you with a myriad of different human relationships. The better you understand and utilize those relationships, the more easily you can take advantage of what they have to offer.

To be aware, yet not judgmental, of other individuals will free you to wing it more effectively. It may sound easy to do, but it is not. That is why it helps to be able to flex your perspective, and see other people's vision of their world.

Sometimes our paths cross briefly. Or, we may parallel someone's path, creating a longer or closer relationship. This is true when we work with others, and when we fall in love.

If you pay attention, you can learn lessons from everyone around you. They may have flown through the same kind of air that you are entering. The problems you face have been faced before. There is intelligence out there. It is within your reach. But you have to understand who has it, where to find it, and how to reach for it.

I flew my glider off the top of Mt Batchelor in central Oregon twice. This is a popular ski resort in the winter. To get to the top, we had to get the glider up the chair lift. Trying to balance it on the chair as we went up was scary enough. Then, at the top of the chair, we still had a two hundred foot climb. At over nine thousand feet of altitude, I was wheezing just to walk. Carrying all my gear to the top would sap all my remaining strength, which I needed to conserve for my launch. The air is thin at that altitude, so launching is much more difficult. At the top of the chair, I spotted some old guy and his wife who were sightseeing. I sauntered up to him and asked for his help carrying my gear up. His wife glared at me, but he helped. I had no scruples; I could ask for and accept help. I knew I needed that help.

You can also learn from others who have differing motivations or cross-purposes. You don't have to like people to learn from them. I learned a bunch from a bad supervisor I once had. I learned how not to treat people. In fact, her weaknesses as a boss inspired me to greatness. However, I got a great zucchini bread recipe from her!

We all have more in common than we have differences, and we are all inter-dependent. The various relationships you create in your journey make a big impact on your success.

Each person you meet is a pilot, flying by the seat of his or her pants. They are doing the best that they can in their own minds. Every personality has a different idea of success. Every one of us has varying motivations and priorities, and we're all on different flight paths.

Some people offer you support, but others don't. They are seeing their world through their own vantage points. In the sport of hang gliding, there are four key types of relationships. These are your flight instructors, other pilots, drivers and spectators. They relate well to the people you meet in the sport of life. We'll discuss each one of them.

Propel Yourself with Good Flight Instructors

Learning any new skill can be extremely frustrating, unless you have a guide. The world is full of people who know more about most things than you do. Enlist their aid in your important endeavors. Find an expert to teach you. Get an instructor, a coach, or a mentor — whatever helps you speed up your learning curve.

You need that expert, outside vantage point. You can't watch and analyze your own launch in a hang glider. Even if you have a video tape of it, you're not objective enough to notice the fine points of your movements. You don't understand how each one affects your performance. This is true in many things. You can't hear yourself sing, for example. Even Pavarotti, the famous Italian tenor, had a coach!

Good flight instructors like to teach. They have an enthusiasm for their craft, and good communication skills. They need to be patient with you, and yet inpatient at the same time. You want to be encouraged when you're down, but other times you need to be pushed. This slight pressure keeps you stretching.

They know the importance of the basics. One singing coach I had made me sing practice scales too much, in my opinion. I hated it. I didn't focus very hard on the exercises. He noticed and asked if I was bored. I replied that I was. Then he snapped, "Well sing them right and we'll move on!" Ouch. Then he softened, "Look, the exercises are easy because doing the basics consistently isn't."

Good flight instructors are rewarded by good student pilots. Your job as student is to review and practice the skills you've learned.

Safety is a top priority in hang gliding, so it should be a top priority for your instructor. You want to feel secure within your level of risk tolerance. There are safety considerations in any endeavor — work or play. Know where the line is for you, and stay just behind it.

Finally, any coach or mentor has to be positive — they have to believe in you, until your belief in yourself takes over. They can see the increments of progress that you're making long before you can. Trust them.

Any important undertaking needs this kind of expert observation and advice. In your life endeavors or in business, you need a mentor. Find a good instructor, someone who will help you grow in the direction you have chosen.

Mentors are everywhere. Be aware of them. Find one. Reach out and ask.

What You Can Learn from Other Pilots

The community of hang glider pilots is like any other social group — loosely linked by common desires. We form a support structure. We provide education for each other. We are inter-related, yet independent at the same time.

The camaraderie between pilots is not unlike the camaraderie between anyone with common interests. Before the flight, there is a lot of discussion, and in hang gliding we call it 'kicking rocks.' We stand around launch and offer up opinions and predictions while we scuff the ground with our feet. Everyone has a different perspective, and everyone chooses to fly based on his or her own judgment.

There is a need to reach a consensus for logistics and the safety of flying together. But deciding where to go or where it will happen takes a lot of dialogue. When you get more than one person, and you have differing opinions — well, that's how politics were invented!

"Mix ignorance with arrogance at low altitude and the results are almost guaranteed to be spectacular."

– Bruce Landsberg

"Hang driving" is also part of the journey. Since pilots are utilizing invisible currents, everyone is guessing about where to fly each day. And frequently there is a lot of arguing, and persuasion going on. Sometimes a group of pilots will drive around from site to site all

Flying by the Seat of Your Pants

day and never find the right conditions — never launch. We call this activity chasing wild geese. Sometimes you don't find what you're looking for. This is not to be judged negatively. It is part of the process — part of reality.

Organizations of like-minded individuals provide knowledge and relate experiences that can help you in your learning curve. Every endeavor has an association. Take advantage of them. In hang gliding, the national organization is United States Hang Gliding Association (USHGA, for short.) These types of groups help filter information for the good of all pilots.

Most activities have a hierarchy. There is a pilot accreditation system in hang gliding, called hang ratings. These hang ratings serve the purpose of getting everyone to agree on skill levels, assign hang ratings to various flying sites and increase the safety of all pilots. Beginners, or Hang I pilots, can take off and land at a low hang site in mild winds. Hang II pilots learn to turn ninety degrees. Hang III pilots learn to make tighter turns, soar, and land on a spot. Hang IV pilots learn to fly in more turbulent conditions, launch from cliffs, and land in tight areas.

Each endeavor has a similar system. Toastmasters clubs have speaking levels. After ten speeches, you attain your Competent Toast Master, or CTM. After another ten speeches that specialize in your choice of areas, you get the Advanced Toast Master — Bronze, or ATM-Bronze. Another ten speeches and a few more hoops to jump through, you get your ATM-Silver. Then, after ten more and leading a series of workshops, mentoring new inductees and you arrive at ATM-Gold. Then on to the Distinguished level. Each plateau means new achievements, new lessons learned.

It helps you gauge your progress as you progress.

Competitions test and recognize skill levels. Some pilots avoid competition. Maybe they don't want to risk failure, or maybe they're afraid that they are not ready yet. But part of being aware is to know where you rank, and compare strengths and weaknesses. I competed many times, as a woman in a man's world. Most of the time, I didn't place at the top. But I'll always remember the time that I placed fourth in a competition among forty men.

"It is a good thing to learn caution from the misfortunes of others."

– Publilius Syrus

The community tracks records held — altitude gains, distance covered, time aloft, etc. My altitude record is fourteen thousand feet, and I flew thirty three miles on that trip. My time aloft record was two hours and thirty five minutes. This sounds good until you find out that pilots have flown over four hundred miles, and stayed up over twenty four hours. One acrobatic wonder pilot made over sixty consecutive loops — yes, in a hang glider.

The few of us women that flew hang gliders formed a tight support system. We called ourselves Women of the Wind (WOW!). In 1979, the three of us (as I said, it was a small group at the time) piled into my Volkswagen bus and went on a hang gliding safari to California. We flew a different site almost every day. It was great fun.

You usually fly with a group of others. The first to launch is known as the wind dummy. They provide a visual indication as to the stability of the air, and the soarability. You can watch where the ridge lift is, or where a good thermal takes the wind dummy. You can plan to head for that same area when you take-off.

A wind dummy shows the way. We have wind dummies all around us, showing us the lessons they are learning. As a speaker, I watch and listen to other speakers. I learn from their efforts and I learn from their mistakes.

Sometimes we have to be the wind dummy — we are the first to take off. We are the pioneer. Different personality styles prefer to be wind dummies. If it looks good, they want to go. They want to be the first. They want to discover the lift before the thermals get crowded with other pilots. They want to be on the top. They are the bolder of the pilots, sure of themselves and of their preparation.

They are ready. They want it. And everybody else wants to watch to see if they make it.

Sometimes wind dummies are in too much of a hurry. They take off before the lift has developed and end up landing early. Then they have to watch the rest of the pilots soaring from the landing zone.

Afterward, there is a debriefing in the landing zone. We compare experiences, troubles and strategies with others as we collapse our wings. Later on — and ever after — the stories are told, and with each telling, they are exaggerated more: "There I was, two thousand feet above take off...."

You can learn so much from others who have similar aspirations. Associate with them. Be aware of them — watch and listen. Learn.

Keep Your Drivers Happy

We all need support people. Hang glider pilots need drivers; assuming the distance they plan to fly is farther than they want to walk back. Drivers are people who drive the retrieval vehicle down from the launch and find the pilots wherever they land. Then, the pilots can simply pack up their gear and either go for another flight, or go for a beer.

"To keep a lamp burning we have to keep putting oil in it."

– Mother Teresa

Drivers may or may not be pilots themselves. Sometimes they are a pilot's friend. They may or may not be interested in flight. Or they might be learning, but not ready to fly at an advanced site. They have to sit around and wait while the discussion ensues at launch, while the gliders are set up, and while the launch sequence takes place. This can take hours.

It is easy to burn out your drivers, and they are often hard to come by in the hang gliding community.

Flying by the Seat of Your Pants

Sometimes it takes two hours of driving on confusing logging roads to reach the landing zone where the pilots landed an hour earlier. Sometimes the drivers get confused, lost or frightened. And sometimes they get mad.

Drivers walk on water — keep your support people happy. Reciprocate any way you can by supporting their endeavors. Drivers volunteer their services. Treat them like heroes. Smart pilots frequently buy dinner for their drivers.

Drivers remind me of the stereo-typical housewives of the 1950s. They kept the home and children sparkling clean. They had a fabulous dinner ready when the "Father Knows Best" husband came home. They were all dressed up to greet him, and had his slippers ready for his tired feet. They listened to the efforts and frustrations of his day. Smart husbands took these wives out to dinner each week!

It's sad when drivers are taken for granted, or treated badly. These people won't be offering to drive again.

It's nearly impossible to over-appreciate your support people. Don't underestimate their importance to your journey.

About Spectators & "Wuffos"

Most sports have spectators. Life has spectators. There are spectators all around you. They watch. They advise. They coach. They question. They pray. They judge. Some of them want to watch the beauty of the sport. Some of them want to see you die. Spectators are not involved in your life, but might interact with you briefly.

Most spectators keep a distance; they want no direct interaction with hang glider pilots. They simply watch until the launch or landing is over. Maybe they applaud. Then they quietly leave.

But there are also the "wuffos," a term contracted from the question, "what for?" Hang glider pilots give this name to the nuisance spectators. Wuffo's are people who come up to you when you are setting up, or tearing down, and ask dumb questions. They say, "Wuffo you do that?" or "Wuffo you don't go?" or "Wuffo you land here?" or "Wuffo you come from?" They haven't ever given the sport much thought, but the beauty and risk of the sport attracts them. They ask uninformed questions, ignorant questions and naive questions. They listen to themselves talk. They distract you. Life is full of wuffos.

"He is the most free from danger who, even when safe, is on his guard."

– Publilius Syrus

Although they are interacting with you, they are totally focused on themselves. They are talking to hear themselves talk, or to impress someone else. They are not there to be of support to you. Remembering that is important.

Wuffos can pose a danger to you. One of my first cliff launches was in California. As I was setting up with a couple other pilots, the usual crowd gathered around us to watch. One particular potbellied wuffo acted as if he knew everything about the sport. As I initiated my run off the cliff, the man grabbed my right wing tip (why, I have no idea; maybe he thought he was helping the little lady). This put me into an immediate right turn in a place where I should have been flying straight off. With a gasp and sudden unknown strength, I aggressively shifted my weight to the left. I recovered, but it could have been ugly. My lesson that day was to be sure you are clear of wuffos before you initiate your launch! Don't let them get in your way.

It is often tempting to get sarcastic, and I have been known to say to hang gliding wuffos, "My mother makes me do this." However, it is important to practice patience and humility. You do not want to give hang glider pilots a bad name. In addition, you never know when a wuffo might turn into a driver, a pilot, or a friend.

Life is full of spectators and wuffos. They are people that are not as aware as you are in your life. Sometimes you are not in the mood for them. But it is important to remember that they are people first, and spectators or wuffos second.

So, be aware of all these different people who surround you. They are on their own flight paths, but some can lend you wings.

CHAPTER 3 – BE AWARE OF YOUR ENVIRONMENT

> *"There is no such thing as bad weather, only inappropriate clothing."*
> *– Unknown*

Weather – The Changing Conditions

The weather is the environment through which you fly a hang glider. It is also the climate in which you live, work and play. It is the present, and the future. It stretches out before you. It is the emotional 'vibe' you sense at work. You can't see it, but you can feel it. It is the economy. You can sense its effect. And you can learn to forecast it.

Many people like to judge the weather. We like to call blue skies "good" and storms "bad." We like to call an up economy "good" or a down economy "bad." However, they are just two sides of the same thing. Besides, our opinion of it makes no difference. The weather, like the economy, just is.

In a hang glider, you fly through all kinds of weather. Wind gusts can pitch your wing up or down, or roll it sideways. You can feel the difference of each effect. You know some of the turbulence is lift, and some is sink. You can learn to react effectively to it.

First, know which way the proverbial wind blows. If you don't understand the basics, you can get in a lot of trouble. This is true in your life journey and your work endeavors, too. What kind of climate are you in? What is the prevailing wind direction? Notice the unseen and powerful influences around you.

The atmosphere has varying pressure and temperature. The difference of these two conditions cause circulation and wind patterns. Add moisture to the mixture, and you get humidity, clouds, fog and precipitation. And storms.

As humans, we exert varying pressure and temperature, too. We individually create our own weather. Collectively we create climate. We can bring a ray of sunshine into people's life, or we can rain on their parade. You've probably experienced a situation at home or in the office where you can feel the tension. This is the weather of emotional stress or conflict.

Wind power increases logarithmically as speed multiplies. A forty mile per hour gust is four times as strong as a twenty mile per hour gust. If student pilots don't understand this, they can get in trouble very quickly. Have you ever endured a stormy relationship? Corporate storms can sweep you away, too. The stronger the storm, the lower profile you want to keep. It's like the bird penetrating a strong head wind.

The difference of the temperature at ground level and at various heights can indicate unstable conditions and a good lapse rate. Typically, air cools as it rises. The more differential, the faster it rises — and the faster you can rise in it. At the opposite end of the spectrum is an inversion, a stable condition where hot air is above cold air, holding it down. This isn't good for finding lift.

Even though we sometimes crave stability, the best opportunities are in unstable conditions. Let's become more aware of the weather.

Meteorology vs. Micro-Meteorology

Our understanding of weather is only a foundation of flight. Just because you understand the big picture, does not mean that you understand the details. Any hang glider pilot knows the importance of the details. In weather, this is known as micro-meteorology.

Imagine water flowing down a stream. If you have seen a boulder in the center of the water, you know that the flow swirls and rotates behind it. Learn to watch for the subtleties of micro-meteorology. They can be powerful forces.

Small disturbances in the wind can be troublesome if they catch you by surprise. Learn to expect them. Anyone who has ever tried to fly a kite probably knows that it doesn't work well behind a big stand of trees. Wind swirls around and rotors over obstacles. It's important to learn to read the terrain of the land, including buildings and

"Each of us makes his own weather, determines the color of the skies in the emotional universe which he inhabits."

— *Bishop Fulton J Sheen*

other structures, and trees. A wind shadow is the turbulence produced directly behind significant obstacles. The turbulence forms as the wind swirls around the obstacle and tries to return to its previous path.

Understanding the weather is much like understanding the average human being. It is handy, and as an average, it is helpful. However, everyone is unique. Each individual human being can be average in several ways, and above average in others, and way below average in still others. You can't be averaged out. Neither can anyone else.

A particular family or business may be experiencing turbulent times, even though the climate around them is stable. Some businesses are doing great in a poor economy. You can always find an example of someone who is performing against the average. This is a microclimate at work.

Some of this turbulence is quite predictable, like the wake you hit when you are flying downwind of another glider. It is similar to the rotor when you drive behind a big truck on the freeway, only you are not on the ground. A rotor from another glider in the sky gives you a quick bump, and then you are out of it. Reacting to the forces within the bump, and trying to correct the navigation is futile, as well as exhausting. Keep your speed up so you don't stall, and just fly through it.

Much of our everyday stress is this way. You can predict its appearance and you know it will give you a bump. Give it a wide berth, if you can. But if you have to fly through it, don't overreact to it. It will not yield you any altitude gain, but you will not lose any either. If you overreact, you will only end up frustrated and exhausted.

You can see a glider coming upwind across your

path, just as you can see that truck in front of you on the freeway. You know when your co-workers are in a bad mood. And you can see stationary objects that might cause turbulence. Don't overreact. It will just make matters worse.

Micro-meteorology means understanding the conditions at any specific location. The wind may be coming from the north. However, if it flows over a headland, it may rotor around and be blowing south on the south side of that headland. The south wind in the rotor is micro-meteorology. Understand that both are at work at the same time.

Your environment has micro-climates, wakes and rotors. Be aware of where they are.

Turbulence, Instability & Opportunity

One of the things students fear about flying is the turbulence. It is like stress, conflict, difficulty, unease and change. They would rather fly only through blue sky — no clouds, no storms, and no turbulence. But in reality, that condition doesn't exist for long.

Turbulence causes your wing to react in sudden, unpredictable and sometimes violent ways. It is unseen. What is it?

It is moving air. You are not flying in emptiness. The air is never still or calm, the way you imagine it on a hot summer night. It is in motion, much like the ocean, or the water in a river. Water seeks to find an even level. It flows to lower areas. The air does the same thing.

The planet is rotating around the sun, and the moon rotates around the earth. Gravitational forces pull on everything. The air molecules are denser in high pressure areas and thinner in low pressure areas.

In an effort to equalize, finding the path of least resistance, the dense air flows towards a low pressure to get a little more room.

Lift and sink result in the process. Thermals are hot air. Hot air rises, and creates a void below it as it does. The pocket of hot air is lift. As the bubble pushes its way up toward equilibrium, the air around it rushes down and around to fill the gap. For this reason, there is sink, or downdrafts, around thermals.

We all seek a comfort level, someplace where we feel at ease. We all try to find an equilibrium, so there is constant motion. And, constant turbulence. Life is unstable. The only constant is change.

"In the middle of difficulty lies opportunity."

– Albert Einstein

Opportunities and threats are just as closely related. They come in a package — together. Sometimes in the middle of our greatest challenge, we find a wonderful opportunity.

The turbulence in the air is unseen, like the wind. But, there are usually clues. Clouds, for instance, are the froth on the top of the air. The more condensed and bubbly they are the more unstable the air. This just means it is moving around a lot due to pressure and heat differentials. If you see popcorn-looking cumulus clouds, you know that the air beneath them is rising. Different kinds of clouds reveal different airflows.

Knowing the meaning of clouds will help you fly successfully.

You can identify signs of opportunities and threats as well. Look for the clouds in your relationships. In your organization. In your life. Disagreements are opportunities to find a better way.

Approaching rain squalls, snow, fog or even sunny patches in the clouds will affect the wind. They may also be clues that the weather will change. This is not necessarily a bad thing. To fly a hang glider, learn to utilize the up air factors, and mitigate the down air factors. In addition, know it is not effective to fight turbulence. The same holds true in your life.

Good things can result from turbulence, as they can come from stress, conflict, difficulty, unease and change. You can use the up air to gain altitude, and fly farther downwind and maybe even set a new record.

You can merge conflicting ideas and end up with a better product. My husband, Bruce, and I built our home this way. We had conflicts and differing opinions — over location of walls, size of rooms and colors of carpeting — during each phase of construction. OK, we had fights about *everything*. And, our house is perfect for us as a result. We still love it. It serves our blended needs. It has withstood the test of time. If we had avoided the conflict, or if one of us had "won," the result wouldn't have been as good.

Use the lift to boost yourself in your chosen direction, or fly through the sink air that life throws your way. You'll experience both — lift and sink — because one can't exist without the other.

You have to practice flying in turbulence. You have to learn to argue constructively. Life is full of disagreement. Learn to expect it, but don't waste your time judging it. You need the experience to be aware of the subtle differences and to utilize the opportunities to your advantage.

Forecasting the Future

We usually leave weather forecasting to the professionals. After all, they have all the sophisticated equipment — the Doppler radar, winds aloft, the computer enhanced ten-day trend. Who can compete with that? Why would you want to?

Because you are more aware of the micro-climate around you, that's why. Your flight may depend on your ability to forecast for yourself. Your risk factor is influenced by your interpretation of the forecast. If the prediction is a tornado, and you fly anyway, prepare for a spinning good time!

Look at the clouds in your life and forecast approaching weather. It is good to have a working knowledge. Barometric readings reveal where you are in the pressure equilibrium of the atmosphere. But there are also gauges for the economy, your business, your education and your net worth. The environment you are in is changing all the time. Learn to read and interpret the data.

"The economy depends about as much on economists as the weather does on weather forecasters."

– Jean-Paul Kauffmann

It is easy to forecast a short term outlook. The farther into the future you try to project, the less you, or the forecasters, are likely to get it right. So, keep forecasting a day or a week at a time.

In the days before the weatherman, farmers and sailors looked up and out to the horizon to do the predicting. "Red skies at night, sailors delight," is quite often true. So is, "Red skies in the morning, sailors take warning." There are all kinds of philosophical old sayings that serve as guide posts for us. Use them.

And use the forecast from your favorite source, but stay aware. Weather predictions can be wrong and timing is frequently off. Keep your eyes on the horizon. Be aware of the world around you. Develop your own forecast into the near future and watch for changes. You'll be more likely to have advanced warning of threats or opportunity. And you'll be able to use it to your advantage.

CHAPTER 4 – BE AWARE OF THE DYNAMICS

> *"Remember, gravity is not just a good idea.*
> *It's the law. And it's not subject to repeal."*
>
> – Unknown

The Forces of Flight

Besides being aware of the weather, you have to understand how to maneuver. There are physical laws that govern you as you travel through your environment. In hang gliding, these are the laws of flight. These laws cannot be debated. These laws cannot be broken. A basic understanding will suffice in your case, but that understanding is very important to your success.

You are flying in three-dimensional air — not just straight ahead, left or right as you do when you drive in a car on a two-dimensional road.

There are four forces working together to allow flight. In a way, they are comparable to the forces in your life's journey. The first force is momentum — your heading or your forward movement. (If you were flying an airplane with power, this force would be thrust.) Momentum is offset by drag, the second force, which holds you back. Drag is the resistance you feel as you try to move forward. Gravity is the third force — it pulls you down. It keeps you grounded. And when these three forces balance correctly the offsetting force, lift, is generated. You gain altitude. You soar.

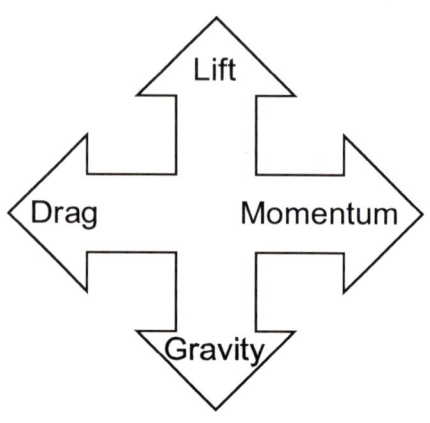

You have similar forces pulling on you in all directions, too. You have momentum — your own energy. As we discussed, the surer you are of your heading, the easier it is to build your momentum. You also have forces that are a drag to you — they hold you back. These may be obstacles, emotions, and negative people. You have forces that ground you. These may be your values, your mission, your passion or your loved ones.

"A certain amount of opposition is a great help to a man. Kites rise against, not with, the wind."

– John Neal

If you maintain the proper attitude, balance, and equilibrium, the offsetting force is lift. You actually create opportunities.

The balance is delicate. If there is too little momentum, you can't produce lift. But with too much, the drag is too great to penetrate. As wind velocity doubles, its force multiplies. This means the drag on you and your wing increases radically with too much momentum or too strong headwind.

Gliding is flying along and slowly losing altitude. A modern hang glider might have a twelve-to-one glide ratio, meaning that when it travels forward twelve feet, it drops one foot. When you glide, it is called a sled ride. Soaring is maintaining, or gaining, altitude. To soar, find and utilize enough lift to stay up. This means to choose the launch time, find the available lift, and take advantage of it.

The weather itself may produce air that is rising, sinking, or flowing horizontally. If you find yourself in rising air, you have the opportunity to turn your glider and stay within that lift. You can rise with it. Pilots call this milking it, and that's what you want to do with an opportunity.

The four forces of flight are the first part of your awareness of aerodynamics. The next is your attitude.

The Attitude / Performance Connection

There is a position for you to fly your aircraft that is the most aerodynamic. At this flying attitude, you are able to maintain control and get to where you are going. You want to be able to penetrate the wind, yet you want to produce the most lift available. To do so, keep your nose attitude into the wind, not too high and not too low.

When you are driving down a highway on a hot summer day, you have probably held your hand out the window in the wind. You can feel some of these forces when you do. First, you can feel the drag of the wind on your hand as you hold it out the window. It wants to push your hand back. You can also feel the lift if you cup your hand slightly and hold the thumb up a little. You are creating an airfoil with the proper attitude for lift. Aim your thumb down to change the attitude, though, and the dynamics change. Your hand dives.

If your attitude is out of whack with the oncoming

wind, you won't perform very well. Maintaining an inappropriate attitude for any length of time can be down right dangerous. Every living pilot obeys this law.

The physical attitude affects the performance of the wing. Your mental attitude affects the performance of your work or your life.

We all bring an emotional attitude with us when we fly by the seat of our pants. If we have a bad attitude, we will probably sink further. Pessimism begets pessimism. If we are too optimistic, we lose momentum and focus. We lose touch with reality. We miss seeing and reacting to problems. A good attitude for life's journey, just as a good flight attitude is just slightly up. Strive for a balanced attitude — neither excessively rosy, nor gloomy. This balanced attitude is the most stable and the most resilient.

Besides, your attitude attracts or repels the others around you who can serve you. Your attitude is a simple choice. It is also an important component in your performance. Be aware of that.

Flight Speed & Momentum

There is a speed range acceptable in flight. Generally, gliders are trimmed to fly within this range. That means that if you let go of the control bar and just hang there, your glider will fly at its trim speed, which is usually set between minimum sink, and maximum glide. These two speeds are only slightly different, but make a major difference in the results you can achieve.

To speed up your glider, you pull your weight through the control bar towards the nose. This puts more weight up front. This is called pulling the control bar in. To slow down your glider, you push your weight back towards the tail of the glider, putting more weight in back. This is called pushing the control bar out.

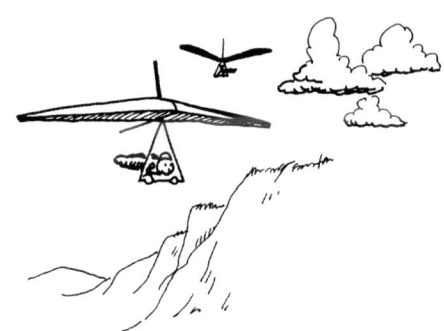

If you fly at minimum sink, you are closer to stall speed. At minimum sink, you are almost floating. Although you have less momentum, you are sinking less than if you were flying faster. Pilots fly at minimum sink on light wind days, when the ridge lift is barely enough to sustain flight. However, they are aware that they are near stall speed and are ready to speed up if needed.

> *"Keep thy airspeed up, lest the earth come from below and smite thee."*
>
> – William Kershner

If you fly at maximum glide, you have more momentum and are nearer to your maximum speed. At this speed, you get the best glide ratio. This means you will fly farther than if you were flying more slowly. If you wander into some sink air, the best way to get out of it is by flying maximum glide.

There is a trade off between minimum sink and maximum glide. If you fly minimum sink, you lose the ability to penetrate and cover distance. If you fly maximum glide, you lose the ability to soar in light wind. You choose the best speed for the conditions you encounter on the fly.

In life, or in work, if you are in good conditions, you can slow down. You can take the pressure off the forward momentum. You can sniff out the opportunities.

You're flying at minimum sink. But if you hit turbulence or threatening conditions, reconfirm your heading and build up your momentum to get out of there. That's flying at maximum glide.

You want to find the best speed for your purposes. Not so fast that you fly through opportunities, but not so slow that you can't take advantage of them. A glider has good control characteristics within the range of minimum sink to maximum glide. So do you. If you are rushing ahead, you might pass by some potential. On the other hand, if you don't have enough momentum, you won't be able to get out of trouble.

Those are descriptions of typical speed range. Outside of that, though, you can run into trouble. A stall in flight is the lack of forward momentum. Since all lift potential depends on a normal flight speed, a stall will decrease your ability to control the direction of the glider's path. You lose directional control in a stall. A stall can induce a spin. On the other hand, a dive is too much speed. A glider can disintegrate at too much speed, just like people can burn out with too much drive.

Aerobatics are performed at both ends of the speed range. For example, a loop can be performed by diving as fast as reasonable, then pushing out until the glider is almost stalled at the top of the loop, at which point the nose points back down to the ground and the glider again gains speed. Other aerobatic stunts include whipstalls, wingovers, porpoising, dive bombing and sideslips. These are performed purely for the fun of it. What's wrong with that? Sometimes you have to stop and smell the roses, or do a few whipstalls!

Your momentum contributes to your forward progress. Be aware of it.

Turning – You Have to be Nimble

We rarely fly straight. We are always adjusting. It is like driving. Although you may be motoring cross-country through the dessert in Nevada on a stretch of road that makes a straight line across hundreds of miles, you don't just aim straight ahead and floor the gas pedal. You make minor adjustments as you correct for changes in the road surface, cross winds, and previous over-steering.

The same goes when you fly by the seat of your pants. You head off in generally the direction you want to go. Then, as circumstances dictate, you make minor adjustments along the way. You keep your eye in the direction of your intended path and move towards it.

Turning, you are constantly changing course, making corrections. You are always searching out the best opportunities. You might see an opportunity to gain some altitude. Stay nimble and flexible so you can utilize them.

In a glider, make sure you are flying fast enough (not stalled) before initiating a turn. The turn itself is easy. Just push out slightly and lean right or left for a right or left turn. Some gliders are responsive. Others are stiffer in their handling and have a lag time, so you will need to initiate the turn before you actually want the glider to turn. In general, the bigger and more lumbering your glider, the more lag time you require to turn when an opportunity or threat approaches.

The Titanic tried to turn when someone saw the iceberg. However, the Titanic was a huge ship. Turning on a dime was not an option. Unfortunately, the turn was not initiated with enough lead time to miss the impact, and the death toll attests to the dramatic results.

Since you are flying in moving air, you will encounter cross-winds that try to push you away from your intended flight direction. In this case, proceed at a crab angle. A crab points where it wants to go, but gets there by going sideways. If you have a wind current coming at you from your left, you may have to point your glider into it, just to go straight.

Sometimes the most direct path is not the straight one.

"Opportunity is lost by deliberation."

– Publilius Syrus

With plenty of altitude, you may want to fly cross-country. In this case, you can turn and fly downwind. Keep your senses aware of lift and opportunities along the way. You use the air to your advantage. Pilots can travel hundreds of miles this way — they turn inside a thermal until they peak out, and then fly downwind until they find another thermal.

Before you turn, look where you intend to go. This is called clearing your turns and is much like looking before changing lanes when you are driving. You want to be sure your path is clear before you commit to it. I used to fly with a pilot who was blind in his left eye. Everybody knew it too, and gave him extra space on that side.

Chapter 4: Be Aware of the Dynamics

Being aware of yourself, those around you, and the physical laws that govern your journey is a non-stop process. You'll never complete this part of the task. But, once you're confident that you have a basic understanding of yourself and you mission, others around you, and the physical laws of weather and flight, you're ready to take the next step — prepare.

CHAPTER 5 – PREPARE TO LEARN

"It's like driving a car at night. You never see farther than your headlights, but you can make the whole trip that way."

– E. L. Doctorow

Contingency Factors

Being aware takes a lot of your attention. Now it's time to fill in the gaps between where you are now, and where you want to go. It's time to learn and grow. It's time to stretch. Preparing is the second of the three elements of winging it.

Preparing a hang gliding flight includes a general flight plan, but the plan is only a small part of it. You don't know what you'll fly into, and how far you might go. You don't know for sure that you'll even make it to the landing area.

Always prepare for more than your plan. If your plan is to fly to a certain field, what will you do if you can't get down? It can happen. What if you end up flying farther than you expected? That, too, can happen. Prepare for all the variables. Have back up plans. Prepared pilots increase their chance of longevity, and success.

The same is true in work, and in life. Preparation is ninety percent, and planning only about ten percent. Preparation has to include all the contingencies that you may need on the fly.

If you are like many of us, you would like the ratio to be just the opposite. You want to set a clear goal and prepare for that, and only that. It would be easier. But, in an uncertain world, just as in hang gliding, you never know. Plan contingencies for your contingencies. You'll use them.

It is important that you include emergency preparation, skills, knowledge, and supplies. Know how to improvise with what you have, if the need arises. Once a friend of mine stalled his take off and crashed below launch.

Actually, that's how my husband, Bruce, and I first got together. We were behind that pilot, each ready to launch, when this happened. Several other pilots went down to help him, so Bruce and I continued to prepare for our launches. This was to be my first high-altitude take-off, and having someone stall and crash right before I launched was making me nervous. I wanted to get it over with, and get into the air.

Then we heard a conversation come wafting up from below, "Tighten up the tourniquet!" Bruce and I looked at each other in disappointment, shaking our heads. We knew that the pilot wasn't bleeding much. We had studied first aid (part of being prepared) and knew a tourniquet was probably not necessary. In fact, it could do more harm than good. We set our gliders back away from launch and made our way down through the boulders and brush to the crash site. The pilot's right thumb was almost completely severed at the first joint. His arm was also broken. He was not losing blood to any major degree and a tourniquet was definitely not necessary. Luckily, the others had put the tourniquet on so loosely that it didn't restrict the blood flow anyway.

His forearm was visibly broken. We needed a splint. Looking around, there was no splint material to be found. However, since he had broken his glider on impact, we fashioned a piece of the aluminum tubing into a splint. We padded it with foam from the vehicle rack. It worked great. We carried him up the hill, loaded him into a vehicle and carted him off to a hospital for some real treatment. All the way there, Bruce and I were in the back with him. Bruce played doctor; I played nurse. My job was to keep his mostly severed thumb from falling out of the bandage. The team at the hospital was actually impressed with the work we did.

We hadn't planned to use the basic first aid skills we had studied and learned, but we needed them that day. Contingencies are like that. You hope you don't need them, but chances are you will. Knowing first aid is a preparation that can benefit you in any aspect of your life. I know people who have come upon car accidents and had to render help. I have met parents who resuscitated a nearly-drowned child using those skills. You might be able to save the life of a choking person in a restaurant if you have the right preparation.

Preparing is an ongoing process. First, plan what, when and where you want to fly. Prepare for getting lucky, yet also prepare for the worst. And have a back-up plan for that. Maybe the wind gods will favor you, and then you have cross-country potential. Your maintenance and care now prepares your equipment for the next flight. Your set-up and pre-flight procedures prepare the glider for the upcoming flight. You check the wind and the weather as you fly and prepare contingency plans accordingly.

Thinking ahead is crucial, there is always a lag time between your thoughts, your input, and the glider's response. Pilots choose their degree of safety margin. A good rule of thumb is to try one new thing at a time. Don't fly with a new glider and a new harness on a new hill.

I learned this lesson again about ten years ago.

A nationally known pilot was at a popular local site and offering to let people demo several gliders he brought. Even though I hadn't flown in a while, I borrowed his new glider, and borrowed a harness and a helmet from another pilot. When I did my hang check, to be sure everything was rigged properly, I noticed I was hanging a little short. That meant I wouldn't have quite as good of control over the wing. Eager to take advantage of the opportunity, I threw caution to the wind (literally.) I stalled my take-off, did a ground loop and crashed into the dune right in front of the nationally known pilot, breaking the glider I borrowed. I also sustained severe damage to my ego. Mother Nature doesn't always remind you gently.

When the outcome is important, restrict yourself to one new thing at a time. Your muscles remember how to fly; it's like riding a bike. But flying a glider, like living life, is more dangerous than riding a bike. Keep your skills current for the sake of safety.

Before every flight, perform a methodical pre-flight of your wing. You want to be sure that it is assembled completely and correctly before you trust your life with it in the air.

Of course, pilots are prepared for the moment. They have the flight skills and aerodynamic knowledge that they need. They also prepare for the best and worst, and make contingency plans.

As a banker, I remember making real estate loans for home construction. Typically, most financial plans included a twenty percent contingency. The amount was never enough. Nobody ever came back and said, "Here's the money back…I didn't need it all." Later, when I made small business loans, new entrepreneurs usually thought they had enough working capital to hold them until their cash flow was positive. Again, it was rarely enough.

Always have a big margin for error.

You do not know what lies in the future because it is a long ways off, and it is hard to predict. So don't worry about a specific plan. If you prepare for various eventualities, then you will always be open to take advantage of the best opportunities that you encounter.

Take Flying Lessons

Learning to wing it may seem to be a daunting task, just like any endeavor you find important. You have to let go of everything comfortable, and launch into the unknown. Unlike learning to swim, however, I do not recommend that you jump in. Sink or swim is one thing; fly or die is another! Hang glider pilots learn their craft in bits. By the time they are flying, they have prepared mentally and physically.

They have studied weather conditions and flying dynamics. They have practiced setting up and ground handling a glider. They have run with the wing on flat ground. And they have taken many ground skimming flights. Each time they stretch a little more. Each time they build their skill and confidence.

You can do the same.

You learn many of life's skills in little steps. You learned to walk that way. You learned to talk that way. You learned to write that way. You want to feel challenged and encouraged — stretched but not threatened. Learning takes place within that envelope.

Remember when you learned to drive a car? It was hard to steer, track all the instruments, watch oncoming traffic and pedestrians, and think ahead. It was difficult. It was scary. Now, you can drive, talk on the cell phone, check yourself in the rearview mirror, and scold the kids — while you are changing lanes on the way to daycare! Well, maybe that's an exaggeration.

What happened? Did the task get easier? No. You just gradually got better. You practiced. You gained skill. You built up confidence and now, it isn't scary any more.

But fear and uncertainty frequently hold you back. Until you decide to challenge them. When you do, your envelope gets bigger. Once you learn the skills to fly, you can fly anywhere. Winging it will be another item in your success bag of tricks — at work and at home.

"He who would learn to fly one day must first learn to stand and walk and run and climb and dance; one cannot fly into flying."

– Friedrich Nietzsche

Stretch Out of Your Comfort Zone

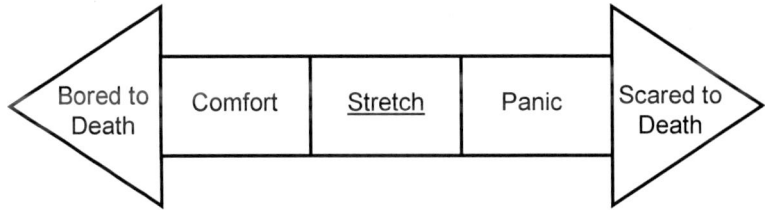

Our learning takes place along a continuum, between being bored to death and scared to death. We have all had experiences at both ends of this spectrum. In between is a comfort zone, a place where we are confident but not growing. Just above that is a stretch zone. It is uncomfortable and unstable, but the growth happens here. Beyond that, we start to panic.

"Some people regard discipline as a chore. For me, it is a kind of order that sets me free to fly."

– Julie Andrews

It's easy to stay in the comfort zone, but real growth can only happen by stretching out of it. The stretch is often uncomfortable, or unsuccessful. So, we revert to the comfort zone until where we practice and we are ready to stretch again. Depending on your risk tolerance, you may choose more or less time in the stretch zone.

As a speaking coach, I know people who panic at the thought of delivering a presentation. In Toastmasters, club members begin by giving an "Icebreaker" speech — one that focuses on an aspect of their personal lives. It is at topic they are familiar with and fairly comfortable for them. Still, it's a stretch. They have to get up in front of people and speak. Once they have that experience, they build a little confidence. So their speech may stretch them a little farther. Maybe they'll talk about something that they have a passion for. As they build their confidence, they progress to speeches that they deliver with more vocal variety, gestures or props.

For some people, the progression seems too fast. They panic when they stretch too far. I always encourage them to go back to an icebreaker topic — talk about something very familiar and interesting to them. They are retreating to their comfort zone, a safe haven. As they develop their skills, this comfort zone will start to bore them. That's when it's time to stretch again.

That's how we learn. That's how we prepare.

Stay Current on the Basics

Another important concept to know is how we retain and remember.

Over one hundred years ago, German psychologist Hermann Ebbinghaus pioneered the study of human memory. In his famous "forgetting curve," he showed that information learned today is mostly forgotten tomorrow. In a month, retention is a mere two to three percent.

By reviewing or relearning skills, we retain and remember them longer before we forget again. Each time we review the material our retention increases.

That is why learning something important needs to be learned more than once. And, we have to keep relearning and applying it. Pilots call this "staying current." The two most important flying aspects a pilot has to keep current are take-offs and landings. Pilots don't have time to stop and think about them as they perform them. They have to be instinctual.

If you want to sing, on the other hand, you must stay current on your vocal pitches, intervals, breath support, etc. These skills seem basic, but they don't maintain themselves — they have to be practiced, just like my vocal coach tried to impress upon me.

To be effective, we have to stay current — we have to maintain our proficiency. In life and in our career, there are basic

"In flying I have learned that carelessness and overconfidence are usually far more dangerous than deliberately accepted risks."

– Wilbur Wright

skills and knowledge that enable us to wing it. Communication, teamwork, leadership, persuasion and conflict resolution skills, for example, must be kept current. You can't wing it if you have to stop and think about the basics. Read articles or books, and take refresher courses.

CHAPTER 6 – PREPARE TO CHOOSE

"One important key to success is self-confidence. An important key to self-confidence is preparation."

– Arthur Ashe

Uplifting Selections

These days, there are so many selections available. The ones you choose now will affect your future success. Every endeavor you undertake, and every purchase you make, costs you either time or money — or both. Don't let your autopilot make these selections for you. Stay in control of your decisions.

If your aspirations are to be a competition hang glider pilot, you need a complete understanding of flight dynamics and meteorology. If you choose to be a recreational pilot, more basic knowledge will suffice.

If you aspire to a job on Wall Street, a Harvard MBA may be necessary. If you want to manage a Wal-Mart store, you may be able to get by with some community college classes and a lot of on-the-job training.

How do you present yourself? Your image tells the world about the selections you make. People make judgments of you in seconds, so make careful decisions. What does your grooming say about you? What kind of clothing should you wear? What does your desk look like? Is your car clean? You'll want all these elements to deliver the same message.

When I started my business, I had several decisions to make with respect to my business cards and stationery design. First, I wanted a professional look and feel, yet I also I wanted something different. I decided to hire a designer during the early part of the process, and do some of the printing work myself to save money.

Do you have a procedure for upkeep? Has time changed the effectiveness of the choices you made years ago? Maybe it's time to make new selections. It's good to review your options periodically.

Don't make choices just because everybody else does. For example, maybe you don't need the latest and greatest computer. If you just need a computer to do simple word processing, you can get by with an older model, and save yourself hundreds of dollars.

Some of your choices are more important than others, but each has an effect on the quality of your journey. Therefore, a basic understanding of your options is important so that you may make an educated choice — one that will serve your needs well.

Trade-Offs in Hang Gliders

Our journey is supported with major vehicles and materials, and there are trade-offs available within those options. If we are not fully aware of our own wants and needs, the choices can be quite confusing.

In the case of hang gliding, the main vehicle is the glider itself. Its framework is aircraft quality aluminum.

The sail is a heavy Dacron fabric. A series of wires triangulate from the end of each tube, giving strength over all. A triangular control bar is attached at the center point of the glider. The pilot gets into a harness and hooks into a loop at the apex of the control bar, hanging inside the control bar.

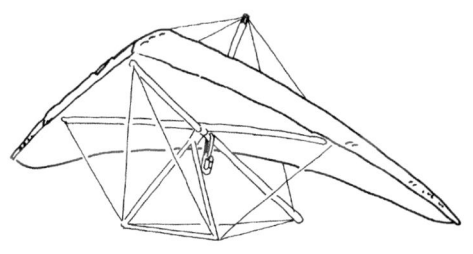

Hang gliders and harnesses have evolved in the last thirty years. They perform better. Gliders glide farther. Harnesses are more comfortable and insulated. Both are also heavier, stronger, and are much more expensive. My first glider cost $630 and weighed thirty five pounds. It came with a swing seat. Current new gliders and harnesses are upwards of $4,000 and weigh over sixty pounds. New gliders are safer than the antique types. There are good used wings that give you a choice in the middle.

"If you are looking for perfect safety, you will do well to sit on a fence and watch the birds; but if you really wish to learn, you must mount a machine and become acquainted with its tricks by actual trial."

– Wilbur Wright

The performance of a hang glider is affected by such things as aspect ratio, billow and airfoil, handling and pilot weight — none of which probably matter to you if you're not buying one. But, your primary equipment decisions will have trade-offs for you to choose between. There is rarely a right answer, only the best solution for your individual needs.

Flying by the Seat of Your Pants

There are always personal preferences that affect your decision, too, such as style and color. There may be differences in maintenance and care, or in procedures. Moreover, there are always price considerations.

I wanted a hang glider that was lightweight and easy to handle. It had to be high performance so I would have a good glide ratio and also sky out. Furthermore, it had to look like a girl's glider. Since I planned to take good care of my glider, it would last a long time. So, price was the last consideration.

You choose options that lend wings to your journey, too. All of the significant investments that you make have various tradeoffs. Consider starting a business. You'll want to understand your needs, for the present and into the future. You'll be putting a lot of time and energy into the effort. You should understand the needs of the marketplace, too. Will your business venture be profitable? Do you have a location that is easy for your customers to find? Prime locations may cost more, so the trade-off is customer traffic vs. expense. Will you be qualified to manage it? Or will you need to hire certain experts to help? The trade-off there is your money, or your time. You may decide to hire a bookkeeper, for instance, if math isn't your strong point. But you have to pay that person. Can you afford the bookkeeper?

If you need to employ staff, do you know how to budget, schedule and supervise them? How will you advertise and promote your business to attract clientele? These choices may not seem as life threatening as choosing a hang glider, but they can affect your health and emotional well being. If necessary, find a mentor, a consultant or business advisor. A community college in your city or county may have resources that will help you make good decisions.

The more stuff you have, the more you are weighted down, emotionally. If bigger isn't truly better for you, then go for smaller. Remember, you have to be nimble to fly by the seat of your pants.

You'll want to put a great deal of deliberation into the trade-offs in any major life decisions. They are the wings that will carry you on your journey.

Safety & Instruments

Besides the glider, you'll need to choose various instruments and gear to take you where you want to go. Helmets and parachutes provide an element of safety. Many hang glider pilots utilize instruments to help quantify and qualify incoming data, such as altitude and lift. They help you steer your craft.

There is risk involved in life — in any endeavor. You need protection. In the early days of hang gliding, we didn't wear helmets. We thought they hampered our ability to hear the wind on the sail, which confirmed our flight speed. Nor did we carry parachutes. They were considered extra weight that would decrease our performance. Besides, we thought we were invincible, immortal. But pilots crashed and pilots died. Some of the deaths could have been prevented with adequate safety gear. So, the philosophy slowly changed. These days, most pilots wear helmets and parachutes. They save lives.

It reminds me of seat belts in automobiles. Old cars didn't have them. It was thought that the big strong car would absorb the shock of a crash. I remember my father putting seat belts into my old Rambler American. Using them was a condition of my driving the car. But they wrinkled my clothes! It took years for many of us to realize that the problem of wrinkled clothing was worth the life saving potential in the case of an accident. Seat belts, like helmets and parachutes, are like insurance.

It is impractical to practice throwing your chute while flying a hang glider. So, when I first got a parachute for hang gliding, I decided to take sky diving lessons. I wanted to have a basic understanding about how parachutes work, so if I ever had to use mine in the case of a structural failure I'd be ready. When you take parachuting lessons, you study the basics in ground school, just like any other endeavor. You practice the body position and timing sequence of pulling the ripcord, although beginners are hooked into the plane with a static line that pulls the chute open automatically. I made two successful jumps and enjoyed the adrenalin rush.

"You start with a bag full of luck and an empty bag of experience. The trick is to fill the bag of experience before you empty the bag of luck."

– Unknown

Many people carry insurance, but that has its drawbacks, too; it costs money. It's inconvenient to have to buy it. It doesn't seem urgent at the time. But, when you need it, you better have it. This is another one of those contingencies that we discussed earlier. Prepare for the eventuality.

Instruments help us track our progress. There are indicators all around us. In fact, there are too many. You can lose your focus if you try to pay attention to all of them. So, a few key instruments can help you along in your flight. Too many instruments are hard to utilize and weigh down your glider.

In the sport of hang gliding, many pilots use an altimeter. This instrument simply tells them how high they are, since depth perception is deceiving at any great altitude. A variometer is another useful instrument to a hang glider pilot. It measures the speed of ascent or descent in feet per minute. If a pilot is sinking two hundred feet per minute, she is in a typical glide path. If she enters some turbulence and notices the variometer is reading eight hundred feet per minute up, she knows she is in a thermal and may bank into a tight circle in an effort to stay within that lift.

These instruments deliver to the pilot important data, much like the driver of a car gets from the speedometer and the odometer. They make the voyage a little easier, and the information easier to interpret. They also enable you to make minor corrections on your drive. You can make sure you're going the speed limit before you pass that police officer!

Another kind of instrument that can give you valuable data to interpret is your financial budget. You can gauge your income and expenses as they relate to your expectations and you can make minor corrections as you go. Otherwise, you can end up bankrupt and not know how it happened.

Like your visual perspective in a hang glider, sometimes your depth perception is off as you journey through life. Choose instruments that help you keep your focus.

Care in Handling & Maintenance

Whatever equipment you choose to fly with, there is always a degree of maintenance and upkeep necessary. In hang gliding, this is a critical issue. But in any endeavor, it's worth your effort and attention. Time takes its toll on everything.

A hang glider is strong in the air; it is fragile when it is on the ground or strapped to the top of a car.

Your wing must be air worthy. Sand and salt water can corrode and compromise the frame work and the sail. On the ground, the glider should be folded carefully so you do not crimp any wires. Wear points should be padded so they do not rub in transit. Most good pilots are methodical about these things. They are protecting their investment. They are protecting their lives.

During set-up and tear down, inspect the wing as you carefully open it and roll it up. Look at it with new eyes every time. Even with the most cautious procedures, things can happen.

Your car will need washing, waxing, oil changes, tune-ups and new

"Another flaw in the human character is that everybody wants to build and nobody wants to do maintenance."

– Kurt Vonnegut Jr.

tires. Your home will need cleaning, painting, and new carpets eventually. Your office equipment will need maintenance, too. It is easy to be blind to these changes — they happen gradually. Perform minor maintenance procedures regularly, or you may have to perform emergency maintenance procedures later.

Those little maintenance things make a difference in your performance, too. Sometimes pilots forget to have spare batteries for their variometer. If you're going to wing it, keep all your equipment and supplies ready to perform. This is important especially when you get high, or the lift is turbulent.

Maintenance can be dreary. It is not the most glamorous part of the flight, that's for sure! But without it, you may have no flight. So make a habit of upkeep. With these preparation procedures in place, you're ready to start practicing!

CHAPTER 7 – PREPARE TO PRACTICE

> *"What is chiefly needed is skill rather than machinery."*
>
> – Wilbur Wright

Ground School

Hang glider pilots don't just fly off a two thousand foot cliff on their first flight. After they are fully aware and have the equipment, they practice at ground school. This is the final phase of the preparation.

Ground school takes place on a little training hill. After learning the set up procedure, you practice running on level ground with the glider in a slightly nose up position. This gives you the experience of keeping the wings level as you launch. At first, it is difficult, awkward. But soon, you can master it.

Then you advance up the hill, but only a few feet, and run down. When you master that, you go up a little farther to start your run. At some point, your feet leave the ground. However, it is more like a long jump than a flight. For these first several flights, you only get a few feet of altitude. This is called ground skimming. At this stage, the rule is "don't fly higher than you want to fall." Start easy to build confidence, strength, and knowledge. As you learn the process of take-offs and landings, you progress farther and farther up that training hill, and gain incrementally more altitude each time.

You have to learn to "flare" when you land, too. This means pushing the nose of the glider up to stop its forward motion. It seems like a lot to think about and everything moves so fast.

Since I learned on a sand dune, I ate a lot of sand — meaning I plowed my face into the dune on several less than graceful landings. This is part of the learning process. Even after all the preparation, you will make mistakes. The learning curve is not smooth. You pay your dues. Sometimes, when it seems like forward progress isn't working for you, revert down the hill.

If you want to learn to sing, you don't start with opera music. Start with a simple little ditty, and learn to master your voice and your breath support. Then, progress to music that is more difficult. When it seems like you aren't progressing (or that you are sliding backwards…which will happen) revert to an easier task. Practice some more. This is how we learn any new skill.

Always stay aware. Visual scanning is important throughout each flight to be aware of other gliders or obstacles around you. Listen to your voice while you sing. Listen to the feedback of others. Keep practicing.

Pre-Flight Procedures

Ground handling the glider when it's set up is much like flying a kite on the beach. OK, it's like flying a BIG kite. The best and most stable place to hold the glider is by the nose wires. Keep the nose of the glider facing the oncoming wind and you will find that you can maneuver the glider quite easily. If it's balanced correctly, it is almost weightless and practically flies itself. Small gusts of wind, however, can make it veer off to one side. So stay aware.

Transporting a glider on a vehicle can damage it. Any dings to the leading edge tubing could produce a structural failure in flight. As you secure it to the transportation vehicle, pad it carefully. Set it up and tear it down methodically, every time. Have a system and use it religiously. You can't afford to overlook anything. Even once.

There was once a pilot in the valley. He flew a popular site for about an hour, and then flew out over the landing zone. He was still over one thousand feet off the ground, so he started performing some wingovers to reduce his altitude. As he did this, he pulled a few negative g's and suddenly his glider folded up around him. He plummeted to his death. I was planning to fly that site on that day, and I arrived on the scene about the time the ambulance was taking him away. I was too upset to fly.

I thought about the glider that he flew. It was manu-

"If you can't afford to do something right, then make darn sure you can afford to do it wrong."

— Charlie Nelson

factured by a company that prided its ease of set up. Indeed, it opened up like an umbrella. It was secured by wing nuts on the heart bolt (the center point of the glider.) I planned to purchase a glider just like his, so I was concerned to know if his accident was a structural failure, or pilot error. I thought about those wing nuts again. If they weren't affixed to the glider, it would indeed fold up like an umbrella if the pilot was performing wingovers.

"Flying is done largely with the imagination."

– Wolfgang Langewiesche

I called the hospital where they took his body. I asked if by chance they had found any wing nuts on the pilot. Yes, they did, they said. They were in the front pocket of his jeans. My heart sank. He had forgotten to put those two wing nuts on his heart bolts, and he didn't notice it in his pre-flight. The oversight killed him.

Then I thought about owning a glider like that. How easy could it be to forget those loose wing nuts? Just the thought scared me. Even though I had a set-up system, I wanted to make the attachment of my wing nuts idiot proof. So, I attached them to a cord that would hang long enough that the nuts would dangle right in front of my face if they weren't attached. I flew that glider for years. My idiot proof system worked for me, and I skied out many times in that glider.

Perform a pre-flight inspection of your glider before each launch. Check everything — it's how to make your set up system idiot proof. Approach it methodically. Look for wear points. Feel the leading edge, keel and crossbar. Sight down them. Look and feel for anything unusual.

Finally don't forget to hook yourself into the glider before launch. I know pilots who hooked in and started to launch, only to reconsider and back off. Then they decided to launch again without re-hooking into the glider. You can't hang on for very long by your hands. Depending on the site, it could be a long fall.

When I launched on the process of writing this book, the details to gather seemed overwhelming. There was so much to think about: how to organize the information, what analogies to use as description, finding good quotes to illustrate the ideas, getting cartoons custom made for the book. And, that was only the beginning. How should I design the cover? Who would edit it for me? What kind of font and format would I use, and what kind of paper? I had to launch a publishing company to publish the book, and I had to get book numbers and copyrights taken care of. Overwhelming is an understatement!

But just like performing a pre-flight, I took small steps. I checked and rechecked. And I made sure everything was set before I launched.

Where ever your journey takes you, be sure you do your pre-flight. Be systematic. Are you ready? Do you have contingencies?

At the same time that you're being methodical, try to look at your project in different ways. Change your perspective and angle. If you always try the same way, you always see the same thing, and always get the same result. Your pre-flight is your last chance before you prepare to run off a real cliff.

Flight Planning

Hang glider pilots only have general flight plans before they launch. In commercial aviation, this is a formal document; in hang gliding, you just tell your driver or the other pilots something like, "I plan to soar this ridge for an hour, and go land in Old MacDonald's field."

However, no pilot would dream of launching without the capacity to do more (or less) than follow the plan. Pilots learn to fly in all situations. They are adept at flying through blue sky as well as storms. They can land almost anywhere.

They plan their flight, but prepare for variables. Sink. Thermals. One sends you down and one takes you higher. Maybe you will gain hundreds of feet of altitude and decide to fly cross country. Sometimes it is easy, and sometimes it is impossible.

Your flight plan is your probable and desirable outcome. An acquaintance of mine planned to become a medical doctor, and did. Then he lost part of his eyesight, which prevented him from practicing his profession. So, he took his medical knowledge in another direction. Today he has a health product store and dispenses professional advice along with the inventory he sells.

Prepare for a wide range, not just your desired outcome. Prepare for several eventualities. You never know where opportunity might take you.

Logging Airtime

You're ready to start flying off some bigger hills, now. You may reach an altitude of twenty to fifty feet. You are going to start logging some airtime! Selecting a site to fly a hang glider involves reading the terrain, considering conditions and looking for potential lift or thermal producers. Selecting your environment involves the same things. You're always looking for potential.

"I learned that danger is relative, and that inexperience can be a magnifying glass."

– Charles A. Lindbergh

You can often tell a good site when you see it. The prevailing wind direction flows up the face of the hill. The launch area is smooth and clear of trees or other obstacles. There is a landing area within easy reach. And, of course, there is potential for ridge lift or thermals.

Ridge lift is produced when the prevailing wind is blowing up the face of a ridge. If the wind speed is sufficient and the ridge is long enough, a glider pilot can soar by flying back and forth in the band of lift at the top of the ridge.

Cross winds occur when the wind does not come straight up the hill. The more cross it is the less likely it is to launch. In flight, cross winds pose no problem, but during your launch and landing, you want to be flying directly into the wind.

Flying by the Seat of Your Pants

Ground school training is only the beginning — flying is how you learn. You can not learn to fly by understanding the concepts. Preparation includes hands on experience. You are not prepared until you have flown. Start logging flights. Learn from your own experiences.

Many pilots keep log book records of their flights. It is like a flight diary. The log reviews the date and time of take off, the place, the glider, the altitude gained, distance flown, and any important lessons learned. This is a valuable tool, because you forget some of those lessons after time passes, and eventually you're apt to make the same mistakes again. You can learn from yourself. You can take your own advice.

Your log book has space for comments. Write down your successes, your failures, your records, and your lessons. Your log book is also a good place to keep any pertinent maintenance records for future reference.

You may want to log your life experiences — successes and failures — in a diary or a journal. Learn from your own lessons, or you may have to relearn them. Become more aware of your own feelings and opinions. This too, is part of your flight lessons.

Are you aware? Are you prepared? You are ready to start getting some perspective! You are ready to grow. You are ready to soar. It's time for a high-altitude launch. It's time to dare.

CHAPTER 8 – DARE TO FLY

"It is not because things are difficult that we do not dare, it is because we do not dare that they are difficult."

– Seneca

Face the Future

It takes courage to face your challenges. The dare is where it all pays off. The dare means pushing your boundaries. It means flying in the face of the fear. The dare means growth. The dare means evolution.

Sounds risky, doesn't it? It is. That is why first you must be aware of the variables and prepare for them.

Many people never fulfill their dreams because of their fear of the dare. The dare is intimidating. The dare is uncertain.

When you launch a hang glider, there is a point of no return. If you are not flying at speed when you leave the ground, you stall. You have to launch aggressively, decisively. Run off the cliff. Launch. Commit.

It's scary, and we tend to avoid being scared. It is dangerous, and we tend to avoid that too. It is easy to stand at the edge of the cliff and vacillate. Circumstances are rarely perfect. It is easy to procrastinate. It is simple to find an excuse not to launch.

I was reminded of that fact as I wrote this book. How many would be authors have their first book, half finished, sitting in their bottom desk drawer? I intended to complete mine, but it was scary. What if I failed?

This final phase of the flying process involves doing it, though. Many would be experts know their craft, but indeed have never actually done it. They 'talk the talk,' but have never 'walked the walk.' I've seen many people like that — pilots, fiancés and business people alike.

The launch is scary. It can be dangerous. "You don't get hurt until you hit the ground" goes the old adage, and you are closest to the ground at launch and landing. Once you're in the air, it's OK. Flying is the easy part.

The dare gives you the experience, and experience is how you grow. You understand the dynamics of meteorology and winged flight. You've trained and practiced. Let go of the comfort of certainty and run into that big question mark — your future.

You can read about riding a bicycle to learn the principles, but to experience the momentum and balance, you get on one and propel yourself. To ride, you must dare.

You can understand the factors required for swimming, but to know how to swim you hold your breath, and jump in!

Any commitment — in life, work and love — is like that. It is never a sure thing. There are many "what if's." The dare means facing that uncertainty. The dare is flying in the face of the challenge.

Push yourself "out of the nest." Take off. Launch.

Be aware while you dare. Look for signs of opportunities. Also, check the view — it's fantastic!

Commit to the Launch

Spend some time at the launch site, looking out at the view below. Get a visual on the landing zone if you can see it. Feel the wind on your face. Search for the potential. Understand what the weather is doing, and predict the best launch time.

I went through this sequence when I decided to write this book. I looked around to see what potential was. I thought about the timing. Then I committed. I told everybody I was launching this project. I regretted it from time to time, too. My friends would frequently ask, "How's your book coming?"

You always get a 'static' just before launch, in two senses of the word. First, it's a hang check done with the glider on the ground to be sure the harness lines are straight and that you have the proper range of motion. Second, it is the last minute instructions or reminders you get from your fellow pilots. They usually give you plenty of static!

Just like the people in your life giving you last min-

"When you stand at the edge of the cliff, jump to fly, not to fall."

– Unknown

ute advice. Or, my friends who knew about this book. I got lots of advice from them, and lots of static. I had to filter through it and decide what made sense for me and my project.

Timing is everything when you launch, whether in a hang glider or any other project. Yet the wind is rarely constant, rarely usual, and rarely normal. It comes in cycles that vary from a little to a lot. It switches from side to side, and sometimes blows up and then down the hill. To launch, determine the optimal timing — when the wind will flow straight up the launch and help lift your sail.

Before the launch, clear your take-off. Be sure that no one and nothing is in the way — around you on the launch, or in front or above in the air. You aim into the wind, for take off and landing. This enables your glider to fly at airspeed while your ground speed is slower. You don't have to run as hard to build up the required momentum.

Every activity has its etiquette. Gliders launch in the order that they are ready and/or their proximity to the launch point. But, just like anything else, everybody doesn't follow etiquette.

Launch potatoes sit on launch and wait through several good cycles and wait for a cycle of perfect air. Their wings block the launch ramp. Proper manners dictate that these pilots back away if anyone else wants to launch.

Different personality styles tend to be launch potatoes. Some people expect a perfect wind before they launch. Unfortunately, this rarely happens. These pilots can miss the window of opportunity while they wait for perfection.

If you're a launch potato, make sure you're not

holding other pilots back. Get out of the way.

To fly, you need a good aggressive launch. If you are not moving at flight speed, you are stalled — out of control. You are still moving fast enough that you wouldn't want to hit anything, yet you are very near the dangerous, sometimes rocky, terrain. You initiate your launch with all the power and momentum you can muster. You only have a few steps to build the required speed. That means committing to it fully, and focusing on it totally. Halfway can be dangerous.

I've counseled many entrepreneurs who wanted to start a business but had only a vague business plan and no real momentum. The likelihood of their success was not good.

Too slow of a launch is called waltzing off. Waltzing is OK if you're dancing, but if you are intending to initiate flight, you better give it some energy. Run it off aggressively — take a leap of faith.

I got a good test one of the first times I launched off thirteen-hundred-foot Dog Mountain, near Morton, Washington. Just as I initiated my run, another pilot's dog came running up to me as if he was chasing a car, snapping at my pant leg. It was too late to abort the take off. Thankfully, I kept the goal of the launch in mind. I didn't quite out-run the dog, and he got one good nip at my ankle. But I kept my focus on running, and my momentum forward. I launched successfully.

Of course, sometimes the decision is not to launch. This is especially difficult because you have come all this way and you had your heart set on it. Maybe the wind is almost good enough, just a little gusty. It is all up to you, and your rationale. It is your responsibility as pilot.

While you are perched at launch and waiting for

the wind to come up just right, you start thinking. You might recall a launch that nearly killed you, or one that scared you. Instead, though, you can visualize a perfect launch — that is the beauty of the mind. I was always afraid to let myself visualize a bad take-off, especially when hooked in and perched at launch. I found I could practice my launch in my mind before picking up the glider and initiating the run. I don't know if visualization works, but I wasn't taking any chances. It always seemed to help.

"There are things I can't force. I must adjust. There are times when the greatest change needed is a change of my viewpoint."

– C.M. Ward

So, why not practice positive visualization all the time? See yourself succeeding in your chosen endeavor. Feel what it feels like. Hear it. Smell it. Taste it. This works for anything you might fear — a job interview, public speaking, going to the dentist, writing a book or starting a business.

Always remember to look where you're going as you take off. Keep your focus where you are headed. This seems so obvious, yet misdirecting focus is a mistake that's easy to make. Your attention has to be on initiating a good launch, not on any peripherals. A pilot I once knew launched off a rocky cliff, looked behind him and focused on his own feet — trying to get them into his harness boot. He wasn't paying attention to where his glider was heading. Before he knew what was happening he had spun around and flown back into the cliff launch. He lived, but his face was ugly for awhile.

Only you decide when you launch. Then do it aggressively and keep your eyes open. Now let's find some opportunities!

Perspectives in Flight

The flight is the fun part. As in life, it's about the flight, not just the landing. It's about the journey, not the destination.

Once you are flying, it is important to stay fully aware and present in the moment. Many gliders have a lag time — in other words, once you initiate a turn, there is a delay before the glider responds. This happens in life and in work, too. That means you are continually thinking ahead, watching for signs and planning for eventualities.

Like the aviation pioneer Andy Anderson said, "Don't ever let an airplane take you someplace where your brain hasn't arrived at least a couple of minutes earlier."

When you are in the air, watch everything around you. Sure, air is invisible. But you do get signs if you tune in. Watch birds, and other pilots. If they are getting some lift, or sinking out, you can get a reading on the conditions. You can take advantage of the opportunities.

Hay is heavier than air, if I remember correctly from science class. Nevertheless, I've seen hay floating upwards past me when I was two thousand feet off the ground. What does that tell you about the nearby air current? It was a thermal. I flew into it, pushed out, turned to stay inside it, and climbed with it. Then I pulled the hay out of my flying wires!

The smell of cow manure can be another sign of rising air. When you are fifteen hundred feet above the cow fields and that smell comes wafting up at you, the air must be rising. You cannot see the air rising, but you can sure smell it. Use all your senses. Pay attention while you're winging it.

I laugh when people tell me they didn't see the advent of computers or the internet coming. True, nobody rang the doorbell. But there were little signs along the way. Some people were aware of the signs and prepared for the contingencies of the possibilities. They were the people who were best able to milk the opportunities that computers and the World Wide Web brought to us.

Focus practice is important. Be present, not flying too far ahead of yourself, or thinking about flying yesterday. If you had a narrow escape five minutes ago, don't waste this moment trying to analyze it. You can do that in the landing field. Focus on the present moment now! You can evaluate later.

I had a good scare at Pine Mountain, a thermal site in Eastern Oregon. I was only two hundred feet above the rocky launch, when all of a sudden, a particularly strong thermal upended my glider from behind and I was pointing straight down at the mountain face below. This is called going over the falls, and happens on the outside edge of strong thermals.

Of course, my intention was to avoid the craggy rocks that I could see below and directly in front of me. An untrained pilot would think that pushing the nose back up would solve the problem. However, I knew that although my flight attitude looked like I was in a dive, I was actually in a stall, and not moving at flight speed. Pushing the nose back up would have exacerbated the problem and probably resulted in blood and gore. So I pulled the control in to speed up my descent towards those boulders! Soon I was indeed diving, straight down. When I could feel the wind racing by my face, I pushed the control bar out, hard. I missed the ground by thirty feet or less. I saved my own life.

"It is good to have an end to journey toward; but it is the journey that matters in the end."

– Ernest Hemingway

My friends (and husband) witnessed this and thought they had seen the last of me.

Being prepared made my knee jerk reaction the right one. You don't always have time to think. You might have to make a decision on the fly. Sometimes you speed up rather than slow down. You want to know what to do in any given situation so you can make a split second decision, even one that may go against your grain.

But, I couldn't dwell on that incident. I had the rest of the flight to seek opportunities. I had to stay in the moment.

As you fly, you endeavor to maximize your potential. As long as there is a driver, some lift and a distant landing area, why not keep going? This is what you've prepared for. You take advantage of the opportunities that you notice on the fly. In fact, noticing them on the fly is the only way to get into them.

When you board a flight to Denver, you never hear the pilot say, "We'll be landing in Denver, unless we find some thermals. In that case, we may go to New York City!"

In business, however, and in life, that's exactly what you want to do. If possible, and if you're prepared, you can take advantage of the opportunity you find in the turbulence and journey farther than you set out to fly.

I set my personal distance records in the Owens Valley of California one summer.

Sometimes you blunder into a thermal. I found a good thermal that took me to fourteen thousand feet. I was level with the snow capped peak of White Mountain. Just Mother Nature and me.

And then, I saw something moving out of the corner of my eye. I turned to look, and there was Bruce! What are the odds of running into your husband in such a remote place? We passed, close enough to yell "Hi, Waugh!" to each other, and flew around together briefly. It wasn't long before we drifted apart again, each following our best course, as we perceived it.

Later, on the same flight, I saw a very small, high, tightly packed cumulus cloud in front of and above me. This was the desert, the valley in California to the east of Death Valley, and it's known for its thermals. Seeing no other signs of lift, I sped up to try to get under that little cloud, hoping for an elevator ride going up. It was the right move. That cloud was sucking like a vacuum cleaner. In a matter of minutes, I had climbed back up to fourteen thousand feet.

For a minute, though, I was concerned that I couldn't get out from under that little cloud. I feared that I would be sucked up into it. I pictured myself as a giant hail ball. This possibility was not one I wanted to dwell on, so I pulled the bar in to my knees, and tried to dive and race out in front of the cloud. Even though I was pointing downward, my variometer indicated I was still rising. Finally, I knew it had outrun its lift when I hit the strong sink that surrounds a thermal.

You can get hypoxia when you fly too high, too fast. Thin air can affect your judgment. Know that. Expect it. When I was at fourteen thousand feet, I continually asked myself my name, what I was doing and where I was going. I made sure I had an answer!

By then, I was very high, two miles above ground level, and my opportunities stretched out below me. With this perspective, the possibilities change. I decided to put some miles in — go cross-country. I chose the path of least resistance, downwind. I cruised down the valley for miles.

Finally, the valley ended in a mountain pass that had severe cumulo-nimbus (thunder) clouds above it. I had already had my exercise with that little cumulus cloud, and didn't want to wrestle thunderheads. I opted to look for a landing area before I got to that point. I saw below me a ranch of some kind, and a few other gliders that had landed there. There was a big flag pole outside the house. Flags are wonderful indicators of the wind, so I decided to land there. The ranch turned out to be a house of ill repute. I had flown thirty-three miles from California to Nevada. The other pilots on the ground warned me not to get to close to the house — the Madame there didn't like women pilots. They were competition for her girls!

If you're aware and prepared, you can go far on days like that.

Some pilots are willing to squeak very close to a ridge to get what little lift is available. Sometimes they are rewarded with great flights. Sometimes they are snagged high in a tree. Others are not willing to play it so close. Sometimes they have to land because they could not stay up. Sometimes, from the landing area, they have to watch their friends who were willing to squeak until they could soar comfortably.

Sometimes you fight against yourself. Take inventory of your muscle tension. It is like driving and giving your steering wheel the death grip. It does no good. Notice those useless and unwanted tensions, and release them. If you don't, they will wear you out. And you won't have the energy when you need it.

Once, I ventured too far into a bowl of sinking air at a little flying site. I knew it could spell trouble. I feared I would hit incredible sink and land short, having to walk out. So, as I tried to fly the glider out as quickly as possible, I kicked my feet uncontrollably (as if that would help.) Bruce and I talked about that one later. Kicking my feet did no good. In fact, it probably hindered me in small ways. It distracted my intention, and probably increased drag. Do not kick your feet in the bowl. It wears you out, and produces no positive result.

Have fun!

Different pilots enjoy their journey in different ways. Early on, I liked to soar the highest. I was light, so it was easy for me to float high above the boys. Those of us who weren't into the extreme aerobatics satisfied ourselves with less radical versions of wing overs, and various porpoising maneuvers in the air. Who needs to go to the carnival and pay for a roller coaster ride when you have your own hang glider?

Or, if you prefer it smooth, you can fly that way. The choice is yours on how you enjoy life. Just take the time to enjoy it!

Now that you have come this far and soared this high, survey your domain! Relish your accomplishments. Reap the rewards. Enjoy the ride. Nobody else can enjoy the view you have right now.

It's a new perspective when you can separate yourself from the boundaries of earth. Your horizons are wider. You'll be amazed at the wonder of it all. It's liberating to fly by the seat of your pants.

Eventually, you have to land, though.

The Landing Zone

Your attitude as a pilot can inflate. You can be carried away with your self importance. You do not own the world. And, it doesn't revolve around you. Landing teaches us that in a variety of ways.

Landing is about the destination. It's about coming back to earth — to what grounds you.

Adjust your attitude when you land — your physical attitude and your mental attitude. When you are coming back down to earth, you are reentering that other environment, where other people are with their own issues.

When you perch back down on earth, you change your position slightly. It is like stepping off an escalator — adjust for lack of forward momentum. As a pilot, pivot to land on your feet. Adjust your body attitude back to vertical-from flying back to walking.

Now it's time to reconnect with the people in the world around you. They haven't been on your flight.

"Angels fly because they take themselves lightly."

– Gilbert K. Chesterton

They may not understand your trials and tribulations, or your elation.

When landing in cow fields, expect cows. This seems obvious, but I was upset when some cows tried to trample my glider when I landed in a field. Then I thought about it. This field was the cows' home. I was in their territory. So, I gently shooed them away, and quickly packed up my glider and got out of there.

Your landings may not be welcomed by others. Your landings may disturb other people. One night at dusk, I was short of the regular spot so I took advantage of a farmer's big back yard. Not knowing if we had permission to land there, and not wishing to have a run in with the property owner, I wanted to leave the premises quickly. It was late, too, and I wanted to get out to the road where the driver could find me. I didn't take the time to tear down my glider, so I just walked it around to the front of the house, hoping I could sneak by any landscaping or fences. When I got to the front, I noticed through the big picture window the whole family in the dining room eating their dinner. From their perspective, they were enjoying a nice meal, and this oversized bird trots by on tip-toes, trying to be discreet.

It's hard to be understated with a thirty-plus-foot wingspan.

Many times, you will be landing in a predictable landing zone — the usual place. You know the terrain, and the prevailing wind. Sometimes, however, you fall short and have to improvise an alternate landing spot. Sometimes you get lucky, go far beyond your goal, and have to land in an unfamiliar place. Many pilots carry portable streamers on thin rods that they can drop into their chosen landing field to verify wind direction.

Preferred landing zones are an acre or two of clear level ground. Sometimes they are impossible to find. Huge flat areas are easy, like open fields or a desert. If the area has a sufficient headwind, the landing can be accomplished in a much tighter area.

Stay aware of trees, fences, power lines, buildings or other big objects and animals. I have landed in a herd of horses and that wasn't fun. So, scope out the landing area. You don't want any surprises on your final approach. Once I was landing on a clear ridge near my home on the Oregon Coast. A motor home pulled in to watch me, not realizing that he was completely blocking my landing. I barely managed to flare to a stop before I flew into their living room.

Stay aware. Watch for wind indicators in the trees. Sometimes there is a flag, a streamer or smoke to indicate the wind direction in the area. Analyze the best approach. Fly conservatively, and a little fast for control. You don't want some little side gust to stall a wing! As you reduce your altitude, keep your eye on the targeted landing spot. This way you can adjust your speed or turns to accommodate as needed.

As you approach the landing area, you make several

turns to reduce your altitude if necessary. You want your final approach to be straight, level, and into the oncoming wind. Focus ahead, where you are going and where you want to end up. You can tell if you are going to be short or over your desired target by how your flight path is headed. Keep focused on the target and adjust speed as necessary. Or, pick another landing spot.

Once you are roughly twenty feet off the ground and flying level, approach your target with additional speed as you enter ground effect. The wind velocity slows down as it nears the earth, which produces this phenomenon. You drop into this layer of slower moving air and you adjust for this fact. In essence, you increase your ground speed, which looks scary. But it keeps you in control.

Just as your momentum starts to fall off, it's time to flare to a stop. You see birds do it when they land on a wire. A flare is performed deliberately and forcefully. You are putting on the brakes. If you have a little headwind to help the flare, you can touch down. If you are landing without wind or (heaven forbid) downwind, be prepared to run off the speed.

The timing of the flare causes many problems in the sport. If you don't reduce your speed sufficiently first, you gain altitude when you flare, and stall (not a pretty picture when you are close to the ground.) If you wait too long, your flare is ineffective and you skid in on your belly (ouch!) unless you can run off the momentum to stop the glider.

Once, we were flying and it got late. We knew our landing would likely be in the dark. The big, flat field would be easy enough to identify, but with the tall grass in the dark, depth perception would be tricky. Knowing when to flare would be crucial, but how would we know we were low enough without waiting too long? We contemplated the question as we set up at the two thousand three hundred foot launch. Suddenly it became clear — push out when your belly skims the grass. The grass, about three feet tall, would tell us when it was safe to flare. It worked, and we all had great landings.

A phenomenon called the whack happens if the nose plate whacks the ground upon landing. A whack is an ungraceful landing where the pilot is OK. (Anything worse is a crash.) Upon witnessing a whack, the other pilots in the landing zone generally begin the duck-like call. "Whack, whack, whack!" The idea is to embarrass the pilot, hoping he or she will work on landing techniques. There is camaraderie and concern in every squawk.

I stalled a landing at Cape Kiwanda when I was learning to soar. I had intermediate syndrome, and was in "push out and soar" mode. I didn't transition to landing mode. I found out what a ground loop felt like. It is a cool, aerobatic maneuver performed completely on the ground — much like a cart wheel. During this maneuver, various glider and body parts may be broken.

So, after my ground loop, I landed upside down. With the weight of my body wrapped around the control bar, the king post slowly buckled. Still, I was tangled in the control bar, unhurt, but unable to move and upside down.

Finally, some nice looking tourist type came running over to help me, or so I thought. Instead, he grabbed his camera and started taking pictures of me — upside down and hanging from my control bar. I started yelling him, but he was so busy laughing at me he couldn't take any more pictures. Finally, he helped me out of my predicament. (And later, he became a pilot himself, and a good friend.)

As you tear down and pack up your glider, you have time to reflect on your flight. How was the launch? How did you perform in the thermals? Did you have any narrow escapes — if so, what did you learn from them? Did you fly with an eagle? Did you witness a beautiful sunset? Did you land where you intended? How was your landing?

At the end of any endeavor, reflect on it. Give yourself a gentle critique of it. You want to celebrate your success, and inspire yourself to try again. That's how you grow.

Reflection is not the same as evaluation. It is not quite as judgmental, although you make judgments. You are always learning to fly. Learning means that you make some mistakes. Reflecting allows you to learn from them, without beating yourself up over them.

Reflection is awareness, and it begins the cycle again. Once aware, you begin to prepare for the next flight. Your preparation begins with the methodical way that you cushion your glider for the ride home.

Finally, let's cap our self-importance. Eliminate some of the drama. Take ourselves more lightly.

I remember a landing after one competition in southern Oregon. I was repacking my glider, and there were several other pilots around doing the same thing. One guy next to me looked at me tearing down and grumbled, "I wish I had somebody to tear down my glider for me!"

I guess he thought I was doing this for somebody else — a man, I suppose. Ha! I quickly thought of several snide comebacks. After all, I had just finished in fourth place, and he was around twenty-seventh. But I always try to keep my humility. Instead, I laughed and said, "Me too."

It reminds me of the calls I got when I managed a group of tourist attractions. They would ask for me by name: Chris Waugh. When Carol, my assistant, said that I was out of my office, callers would ask, "When will he be back?" Same thing — you want to say something snide to put them in their place. But not Carol. She'd just say, "She'll be back at three thirty."

"The probability of survival is inversely proportional to the angle of arrival."

– Unknown

It is important to keep your sense of humor on your journey — you'll need it! You need it at work. You need it with your relationships. You need it every day of your life. We tend to over-dramatize our own slights.

We all have to land eventually. It's the end of another leg of our journey. And it's the beginning of the next one.

FLYING HIGH

> *"The good life is a process, not a state of being. It is a direction not a destination."*
>
> *– Carl Rogers*

Soar to New Heights

So, off you go! Life is an extreme sport, just like hang gliding. It is turbulent and it can be scary at times. It is full of lift and sink — opportunities and threats. It can be unpredictable. But, the opportunities are endless, even though they may be hard to identify.

Resist the desire to try to control everything in your life. You can't anyway, and you'll just exhaust yourself. You can't always plan the specific success that lies before you. Instead, keep your options open and look for the opportunities that you're flying by today.

Living life on the fly is easy. It's exhilarating. Just remember:

Be Aware — don't skimp on this part. Endeavor to understand your own values, motivations and desires. Know that others around you are operating with their own agendas. Some offer help and others don't. Forget how things "ought to" be and deal with the laws of the environment and the dynamics of your flight. You will start to identify lift in the turbulence — these are opportunities.

Prepare — learning is an ongoing process. Put time into getting yourself ready to take advantage of the lift in the turbulence of your life. Consider the trade-offs in the options you choose. Practice with the equipment that will carry you forward. Make little test flights at ground school, and learn from each one. Start logging some airtime.

Dare — commit to launch into your future. You can't stay grounded anyway, so don't try. Instead, aggressively embrace the changing climate. Sure, it's scary at first. The dare, however, is how you grow. It is how you build confidence and learn. It's how you succeed. The flight is the fun part. That's where you find the opportunities, and see the sights. Touch down gently when you land. Take yourself lightly.

Learning to wing it is an upward spiral — not a line with a beginning and an end, and not a mere cycle. It is a progression. It's your evolution. Like the world around us, our lives are full of spirals, and so is our learning to fly. We have ups and downs, and turbulence, just like the wind.

We have to clear up the misconception that flying by the seat of your pants is a bad thing. We have to become opportunity seekers instead of goal seekers. There is a world of possibility out there if we stay open to it.

Most success gurus tell us that we have to set concrete goals, complete with details and dates. They say it's the only way we'll know if we succeed or not. But, first of all, our future isn't always concrete, clear and detailed. We don't have a crystal ball! Secondly, our judgment of success is made in the end, not the beginning. We don't have to reach every goal we set to be successful.

It's much better to stay nimble in a world of change and uncertainty. So, plan what you can. But when you're uncertain about a specific outcome, choose a direction and wing it.

Whether or not you practice the skills to succeed on the fly, your life will fly by. Flying through uncertainty can be a great teacher. It's a great confidence builder. You live to evolve — for yourself and human kind. Choose to soar!

Lending Wings to Others

Are you a leader?

If so, become the flight instructor for your team.

Develop a group focus as a team and discuss your common mission frequently. Do this in meetings, and even over the water cooler. Everyone must agree on the heading, just like a flock of geese. All the momentum must be pulling in the same direction. Encourage the various perspectives that individuals bring to the group. These diverse dynamics keep the group strong and resilient. Talk about the limitations of the group. Those can include money, talent or even drive.

"There's no such thing as a natural-born pilot."

— Chuck Yeager

"What kind of man would live where there is no daring? I don't believe in taking foolish chances, but nothing can be accomplished without taking any chance at all."

– Charles A. Lindbergh

Agree on the degree of risk tolerance that is acceptable within the team for maximum performance. Finally, make each pilot individually responsible. Don't take their credit and don't cover their mistakes.

They also need to understand the competition. What successes and failures have similar teams faced, and what can be learned from that? Who can be a resource to the group — teachers, trainers, mentors? Make sure that they understand the needs of their own drivers, those important people who support them on their journey. And, teach them how to deal with those pesky wuffos.

Discuss the conditions and the variables of the business climate that they will encounter. Talk about upcoming forecasts in the economic conditions, for example. And strive to keep the momentum and attitude of the group in balance so that lift can be produced.

The team must be aware to fly by the seat of their pants.

You have to prepare your people. Make them stretch out of their comfort zone often. Keep them current on the basic and critical skills that they need to be effective. As the leader, you can't be directing people every minute. Just as the flight instructor does after ground school, you have to let go. Make sure that they have the tools they need — the wings, the safety gear, and the instruments — to succeed in flight. Maintain and update equipment so that the team is always prepared to wing it. Set up procedures that eliminate as many threats as possible. And make them practice. Prepare them for the expected results, and for the inevitable contingencies.

Keep them prepared.

Encourage them. Give them the confidence to dare. Then, shove them out of the proverbial nest! Let them experience the wonders of flight. Let them sniff out and take advantage of opportunities on the fly. And, as a group, reflect upon the results in the landing zone.

Let them dare. Encourage them to dare.

As your people grow, so will your organization. It, too, can soar.

About the Author

Chris Waugh is the President of reNvision, Inc. She is a motivational speaker, corporate trainer, author and management consultant, and works with groups of business professionals who want to learn how to fly by the seat of their pants. She helps them identify the opportunities that lie before them, and prepares them to take full advantage.

Her motivating keynote presentations stimulate hope and action in her audiences. She uses her experiences in business and in adrenalin sports to illustrate how to navigate the wild world of work. Yet, she maintains that these skills are safe to try at home.

Her *Touch & Go Training* sessions are interactive and fun. Participants revitalize the skills that they need to be effective. She specializes in fresh perspectives of the basics, such as goal setting, time management, stress & conflict, personality predicaments, communication, sales, service, supervision, motivation and teamwork.

She writes articles for magazines and newsletters, and publishes a monthly E-zine, *On the Fly*.

Her business background spans thirty years of leadership and management in a variety of industries — banking, tourist attractions, restaurants, retail, manufacturing, services and non-profit organizations. She developed her leadership style and passion for employee development, to which she credits the success of her business endeavors.

She is an advanced hang glider pilot and a charter member of the United States Hang Gliding Association.

Chris is a professional member of the National Speakers Association, and an Advanced Toastmaster in Toastmasters International.

You can find out more about Chris, her business and her expertise — and also order more copies of "Flying by the Seat of Your Pants" — at her website:

http://www.reNvision.com